WHERE ANGELS FEAR TO TREAD

A Play in Two Acts

by

ELIZABETH HART

Based on the novel by
E. M. FORSTER

Italian dialogue by Gita Denise

SAMUEL   FRENCH

LONDON

Copyright © 1963 by E. M. Forster and Elizabeth Hart
All Rights Reserved

WHERE ANGELS FEAR TO TREAD is fully protected under the copyright laws of the British Commonwealth, including Canada, the United States of America, and all other countries of the Copyright Union. All rights, including professional and amateur stage productions, recitation, lecturing, public reading, motion picture, radio broadcasting, television and the rights of translation into foreign languages are strictly reserved.

ISBN 978-0-573-01477-2

www.samuelfrench.co.uk
www.samuelfrench.com

For Amateur Production Enquiries

United Kingdom and World
excluding north america
plays@samuelfrench.co.uk
020 7255 4302/01

Each title is subject to availability from Samuel French, depending upon country of performance.

CAUTION: Professional and amateur producers are hereby warned that *WHERE ANGELS FEAR TO TREAD* is subject to a licensing fee. Publication of this play does not imply availability for performance. Both amateurs and professionals considering a production are strongly advised to apply to the appropriate agent before starting rehearsals, advertising, or booking a theatre. A licensing fee must be paid whether the title is presented for charity or gain and whether or not admission is charged.

The Professional Rights in this play are controlled by Samuel French Ltd, 24-32 Stephenson Way, London NW1 2HD.

No one shall make any changes in this title for the purpose of production. No part of this book may be reproduced, stored in a retrieval system, or transmitted in any form, by any means, now known or yet to be invented, including mechanical, electronic, photocopying, recording, videotaping, or otherwise, without the prior written permission of the publisher. No one shall upload this title, or part of this title, to any social media websites.

The right of E. M. Forster & Elizabeth Hart to be identified as author of this work has been asserted in accordance with Section 77 of the Copyright, Designs and Patents Act 1988.

NOTES

The action should move as quickly and fluidly as possible, avoiding inter-scene curtains, making use instead of dim-outs and where indicated, music.

Since Italy pervades the major part of the Play and influences its development, the views from Gino's loggia and from the windows of the Hotel Stella d'Italia are important and should dominate their respective sets.

WHERE ANGELS FEAR TO TREAD

Presented by Tennent Productions Ltd and John Gale Productions at The New Arts Theatre, London, on the 6th June 1963, and subsequently at the St Martin's Theatre, on the 9th July 1963, with the following cast of characters:

(in the order of their appearance)

IRMA HERRITON	Mary Williams
HARRIET HERRITON	Nan Munro
MRS HERRITON	Violet Farebrother
PHILIP HERRITON	Michael Denison
CAROLINE ABBOTT	Dulcie Gray
SIGNORA ALETTI	Gita Denise
CAB DRIVER	Andreas Malandrinos
GINO CARELLA	Keith Baxter
PERFETTA	Daphne Newton

Directed by GLEN BYAM SHAW

Décor by Motley

SYNOPSIS OF SCENES

ACT I

SCENE 1 A room in Mrs Herriton's house, Sawston, Surrey. 9 a.m. on an August morning, in the year 1906

SCENE 2 The salone of the Hotel Stella d'Italia, Monteriano, Italy. A week later. About 10 p.m.

SCENE 3 Gino Carella's house, Monteriano. The following morning

ACT II

SCENE 1 The salone of the hotel. Noon, two days later

SCENE 2 The same. 11.15 p.m. the same night

SCENE 3 Gino's house. Half an hour later

SCENE 4 The salone of the hotel. Morning, two weeks later

ACT I

Scene 1

SCENE—*A room in Mrs Herriton's house, Sawston, Surrey. 9 a.m. on an August morning, in the year 1906.*

Neither a study nor a drawing-room, it is a place where Mrs Herriton writes her letters, entertains intimates at tea, gives her orders to the staff and conducts all really private tête-à-têtes with members of her family. The décor is Edwardian. The walls have panels, filled with eau-de-nil damask; the floor flowers with an Aubusson. On the desk and the several small tables are photographs in silver frames and the tables are also laden with fragile knick-knacks, snuff-boxes, smelling-salts bottles, etc. The total effect has a period charm and should evoke a smile, but not ridicule. Nor does the room seem oppressive at first, it is only later that all these objects, each in its proper place, each dusted and polished to perfection begin to weigh on one; and that the flawless order, the correct taste, the lack of a single revealing idiosyncrasy begins to cloy. There is an arch up LC leading to the hall and other parts of the house and an exit down L leading to the garden. Down R there is a shallow alcove in which stands a luxuriant potted palm. In front of this stands a revolving bookcase. Up RC is a writing-desk with a chair beside it. A small oval table stands up LC, R of the arch. Blue velvet curtains hang in the arch. Down L there is a mahogany Victorian armchair with a mahogany Victorian work-table L of it. Another mahogany Victorian armchair is RC with a low, Moorish table R of it. A footstool is down C. A potted palm stands on a low table against the wall L. There are rugs on the floor and gold-framed pictures on the walls.

When the CURTAIN *rises, the stage is empty. Almost immediately the ordered tranquility is disturbed by a woman's voice rising in fury outside in the hall.*

HARRIET (*off; shouting*) Give it here! (*Closer*) Give it here, at once, you wicked girl!

(IRMA HERRITON *runs on through the arch. She is aged ten, ordinarily a rather subdued child. But now, excitement has made her vivid. She clutches a large, tinted picture postcard to her bosom, as a priest pursued by a horde of infidels would clutch a sacred relic*)

IRMA (*as she runs in*) Grannie! Grannie! (*She runs* C, *looks around, sees the room is empty and runs down* R)

(HARRIET HERRITON *plunges in through the arch. She is a spinster in her forties, large, plain and clumsy. She crosses to* L *of the armchair* RC)

(*To Harriet. Defiantly*) It's not yours, Aunt Harriet! It's addressed to me. (*She holds up the card, looking at the back of it*)

HARRIET (*lunging below the armchair* RC *to Irma*) I forbid you to read it!

(IRMA *skips agilely round the furniture, reading the message on the card aloud, always keeping just out of reach of* HARRIET, *who pursues her, with the effect of a grotesque "Ring a Ring of Roses".* IRMA *goes above the armchair to* L *of the footstool* C. HARRIET *follows above the armchair* RC *to* R *of the footstool* C)

IRMA (*reading*) "Love and kisses from your little brother, Vittorio." (*She stands stock-still, incredulous*) My little brother! (*To Harriet. Excitedly*) I didn't know I had one.

(HARRIET *snatches the postcard and tears it in pieces*)

(*She crosses below Harriet to* R *of her, trying to reach the postcard*) Stop! It's mine! (*She catches at Harriet's arm, her voice rising in shocked anger*) That's stealing! You could be put in prison.

(HARRIET *slaps Irma's wrist.* IRMA *bursts into loud sobs and moves down* R.

MRS HERRITON *enters down* L *from the garden. She is in her late sixties, but there is nothing of the stock dowager about her. Her figure is trim and she manages to look well-groomed, even in gardening gloves and an old straw hat. It is hard to imagine a situation that would cause her to raise her voice or forget the tact for which she is locally celebrated. She is carrying a basket of cut flowers and a pair of cutters. She takes in the troubled domestic scene with one glance.* HARRIET *drops the pieces of the card to the floor, near the footstool*)

MRS HERRITON (*moving down* C; *in a low, tranquil voice, with the undertone of final authority*) What is the matter, Harriet? Irma, why are you crying?

IRMA (*crossing below Harriet to* R *of Mrs Herriton*) Aunt Harriet slapped me, Grannie, and . . .

HARRIET ⎱ (*together*) ⎰ She deserved it, Mother. (*She moves to* R *of Irma*) She was impertinent and disobedient to . . .

IRMA ⎰ ⎱ I only tried to read my postcard. (*She points to the pieces on the floor*) She tore it all . . .

MRS HERRITON (*holding up a hand*) One at a time, dears. (*She moves unhurriedly to the desk, puts the basket and cutters on the desk chair, removes her hat and puts it on the right end of the desk*)

(IRMA *subsides into sniffles,* HARRIET *into glowering silence.* IRMA *crosses to* L *of Mrs Herriton.* HARRIET *crosses down* R)

(*She turns to Irma and takes a snowy handkerchief from her belt. Gently*) Irma, never wipe your eyes on your sleeve. It looks common and it's not hygienic. (*She hands the handkerchief to Irma*)

IRMA. Thank you, Grannie.

To face page 2—Where Angels Fear to Tread

Photograph by Angus McBean

MRS HERRITON. "Grandmother", dear. (*She removes her gardening gloves and puts them on the right end of the desk*)

(IRMA *wipes her eyes and returns the handkerchief to Mrs Herriton*)

IRMA. Grandmother, who is my little brother Vittorio?

(MRS HERRITON *moves* C *and looks at Harriet*)

Why has no-one ever told me about him? (*She moves to* L *of Mrs Herriton*) Why does Aunt Harriet hate him?

HARRIET (*moving* RC) I don't hate him. I pity him from the depths of my heart.

MRS HERRITON. Harriet!

(HARRIET *stops, looking guilty*)

I think you had better tell me just what happened.

HARRIET. It was really the fault of that new postman. Officious fool! I heard him tell Irma that someone had sent her a postcard from Italy and before I could stop him he had handed it to her. I ordered her to give it to me, but instead, she . . .

MRS HERRITON (*interrupting; tone and glance convey that she knows Harriet has bungled the whole thing*) I see. What was the message?

HARRIET. Some silly nonsense, pretending to have been written by the baby himself.

IRMA. It was *not* nonsense! (*She jumps eagerly up and down,* L *of Mrs Herriton*) Does she mean my brother didn't write it himself? Is he a really *little* baby, then?

(MRS HERRITON *takes* IRMA'S *hand, and pushes her gently on to the footstool, then crosses to the armchair* RC)

MRS HERRITON. Let's sit down quietly, dear, and grandmother will explain everything. (*She sits in the armchair*) Harriet, would you mind taking those flowers to the pantry, before they wilt?

(HARRIET, *recognizing that she is being dismissed in disgrace, moves sullenly to the desk and picks up the basket of flowers*)

Don't try to arrange them, I'll do that later. Fill the sink a quarter full and lay them in gently. Try not to break the stems or knock off the petals.

HARRIET. Since you think I'm so clumsy, I'll ask cook or Nora to see to them.

(IRMA *picks up the pieces of postcard from the floor*)

MRS HERRITON. Seeing to the flowers is not one of cook's duties and this is Nora's morning to clean the silver. We have no trouble with the servants, dear, because I take pains to upset their routine as little as possible; I understand that their natures are not flexible.

HARRIET. Oh, very well. (*She moves to the arch then stops and turns. With genuine dignity*) I think it's only fair, Mother, for you to correct

Irma's impression that I hate the Carella baby. You know that I pray for it every night.

(HARRIET *exits through the arch*)

IRMA. Carella? Isn't that the name of my new father?

MRS HERRITON. Your father's name was "Charles Herriton". You never had and can never have a "new" one.

IRMA. But when mamma wrote and said that she had married an Italian nobleman . . .

MRS HERRITON. Signor Carella is not a nobleman. And he is nothing to do with you. He was your poor mother's second husband and now she is dead, he is not even a connection.

IRMA. Oh. (*She looks at a rather large fragment of postcard in her hand, then lights up with recognition*) "Monteriano"—that's the place where she used to live.

MRS HERRITON. Yes, dear. She lived there because it was Signor Carella's home. She met him there while she was visiting Italy. (*She takes the pieces of card from Irma*) After they had been married about a year . . .

IRMA. They had a baby. My little brother Vittorio.

MRS HERRITON. Your half-brother. It is not quite the same. (*She puts the pieces of card on the table* RC)

IRMA (*paying no heed to the dampening qualification*) But why didn't mamma ever write to me about him? Why didn't she send me his picture? (*She rises*) I do think it was mean of her. (*She turns up* C)

MRS HERRITON (*catching Irma's arm and drawing her close*) Your mother died when he was born. She never even saw him.

IRMA. Never even saw . . . Oh, poor mamma! Poor, poor . . . (*She dissolves into the sort of gentle tears that can be observed in the audience at any sad film*)

MRS HERRITON (*patting Irma comfortingly*) Dear little Irma. I knew how this would distress you and that is why I have not told you before.

(PHILIP HERRITON *enters through the arch, hesitates, then remains in the archway, unobserved by* IRMA *and* MRS HERRITON. PHILIP *is in his late thirties, with features that are a curious blend of good and bad. He has a fine forehead, a large well-shaped nose, eyes that reveal observation, humour and sympathy, but people who believe destiny resides in the mouth and chin shake their heads when they look at him: both are irresolute. He carries an unlighted cigarette in a holder*)

I felt that your mother's death was a cruel enough blow for a little girl. To tell you how she died, as well, would have made it almost more than you could bear. So now you see why we have all kept silent about the baby until now.

(MRS HERRITON *delivers this amazing tissue of illogic, half-truths and falsehood, with such wise and tender concern that* PHILIP *gives a smile of cynical admiration as he listens.* IRMA *responds to Mrs Herriton's last statement with a nod and a final sob*)

IRMA. Yes, Grandmother. (*She starts to wipe her eyes on her sleeve, remembers and checks herself*) May I have your handkerchief again?

(MRS HERRITON *hands her handkerchief to Irma, turns and sees Philip*)

PHILIP (*moving down* LC) Am I intruding, Mother?
MRS HERRITON. Not at all, Philip. Irma and I have been having a serious talk, but we are finished now.

(IRMA *returns the handkerchief to Mrs Herriton*)

PHILIP. Yes, Harriet told me that the cat was out of the bag—or rather the kitten.

(IRMA *laughs. Having paid her respects to tragedy, she has dismissed it totally*)

IRMA (*moving to* R *of Philip*) Have you seen him, Uncle Phil?

(PHILIP *shakes his head.* MRS HERRITON *arranges the pieces on the table* RC, *to re-form the picture*)

Do you suppose he looks like the baby in that Italian picture over your desk?
PHILIP. Very probably. Most babies in Italy look like Bellinis when they don't look like Della Robbias.
IRMA. He must be adorable. I can hardly wait to see him. Do Italian babies wear bootees?
PHILIP. Irma, I am an ignorant bachelor. I don't even know what bootees are.
IRMA. They're a kind of sock of lovely soft wool, Uncle Phil. (*She turns to Mrs Herriton*) I should love to knit him a pair.

(PHILIP *takes matches from his pocket and lights his cigarette*)

MRS HERRITON. Then why don't you, dear? Aunt Harriet is going to the library and there's that shop just across the road that sells very nice wool. Tell her I would like her to take you there after she has changed my books.
IRMA. Thank you, Grandmother. How long ago exactly did mamma die?
MRS HERRITON. Just a little over four months.
IRMA (*with enormous satisfaction*) Then he is still quite tiny. I'll be able to pick him up and carry him about. I'll be able to give him a bath.

(IRMA *finds the last prospect is so blissful that she breaks into an exuberant skip, begins a rendition of "Rock-a-bye Baby" and exits through the arch*)

PHILIP (*crossing above the armchair* RC *to the revolving bookcase* R)

Children are nothing if not practical. (*He puts the spent match in the ashtray on the bookcase*) One can't do anything with a dead mother, but a living brother one can bath and knit socks for. Do you really mean to let her send them to him?

MRS HERRITON (*rising and crossing to the work-table* L) My dear Philip, have you ever looked at Irma's knitting? (*She takes some sewing, a threaded needle and a thimble from the work-table*)

PHILIP. Not with passionate attention.

MRS HERRITON. She spends most of her time pulling out what she's done wrong. (*She sits in the armchair* L, *takes her glasses from the case hanging at her belt, and puts them on*)

PHILIP (*crossing to* L *of the armchair* RC; *with an appreciative smile*) Ah! So the socks will be like Penelope's web?

MRS HERRITON. Exactly. (*She sews*) But if she thinks she's making something for the baby, her impatience to see him may be a little —a *very* little curbed. (*She sighs*) If we could only have kept her from finding out until she was a few years older. She is just at the age when baby-worship is a cult with little girls. They all go through the phase. Harriet was positively idolatrous of you.

PHILIP. I don't believe it. If Harriet ever hung over my cradle it was to tell me gluttony was a sin and snatch away my bottle.

(MRS HERRITON *smiles for a moment*)

MRS HERRITON (*seriously*) Poor Harriet! She seems less and less able to control her temper, and when she loses it she loses all judgement as well. She mismanaged the whole affair of that—(*she indicates the pieces of the postcard*) wretched postcard.

(PHILIP *moves to the table* RC, *kneels above it and studies the pieces of postcard with nostalgia*)

PHILIP. It must be the view of the battlements and towers from the valley. Not a bad photograph in black and white. But naturally he'd buy the tinted version. (*He rises*) Why do you suppose he sent it?

MRS HERRITON. Perhaps he is finding it difficult to manage with only the little Lillia was able to leave him. He may hope that if he stirs up Irma, she will plague us into taking the baby off his hands.

PHILIP. For a suitable amount of cash?

(MRS HERRITON *nods*)

(*He laughs*) A naïve hope.

MRS HERRITON. Irma *will* plague us, you know. We are in for a very trying period. I warned you that we should be.

PHILIP. You did, indeed. That's how you won me over to hushing up the baby's existence. (*He moves* C. *Wryly*) I'm the unheroic type who will pay any price for peace.

MRS HERRITON. What "price" have you paid for keeping silent for a few months about something that was no-one's concern but our own?

PHILIP. Well, I've read somewhere that secrecy is bad for the soul. And we do seem to have gone in for rather a lot of it. We put Irma off with excuses for not sending her out to her mother in Italy. We put Lillia off . . .

MRS HERRITON. I needed no excuses for keeping my granddaughter from an environment that was sure to harm her. When Lillia married that man, she lost all moral right to bring up Irma. And I think she knew it.

PHILIP. At any rate, she would never have dared to oppose you a second time. I doubt if she'd have done so the first, if sweet respectable Caroline Abbot hadn't been there to give her support and encouragement.

MRS HERRITON. Caroline has been behaving very tiresomely lately.

PHILIP. She's a tiresome person. (*He moves to the desk chair and sits*) That's why her conduct over Lillia's marriage is such a fascinating riddle to me. Worthy, conventional Caroline, assisting a romance between a cheap Italian fortune-hunter, the son of a village dentist, and a woman who, for all her silliness, was at least a lady.

MRS HERRITON (*impatiently*) Caroline's past conduct doesn't matter; her present attitude does. I'm glad she is going away for a holiday just now. Irma's nagging will be bad enough; with Caroline as her ally, we should have no peace at all.

PHILIP. Her ally? Irma's ally? I don't understand. You *can't* mean that she's been nagging you to take that blasted baby?

MRS HERRITON (*nodding*) Uh-huh!

PHILIP (*rising*) But that's the most colossal cheek I ever heard of. (*He moves* RC) She must be barmy. Why didn't you tell me? I'd have sent her about her business.

MRS HERRITON. It's a situation that requires extremely delicate handling, Philip. Caroline is . . . (*She breaks off*)

(HARRIET *enters through the arch. She is wearing her hat and carries her handbag. She has recovered from her sulks and looks almost amiable*)

HARRIET (*moving to* R *of Mrs Herriton*) Irma says you've given her permission to choose wool and a bootee pattern, Mother.

MRS HERRITON. That's correct. (*She rises, puts her sewing in the work-table, crosses and sits in the desk chair*)

HARRIET. I just wanted to make sure. It's a kind idea, to send the poor baby socks. I'm sure that dreadful man lets it go barefoot.

(MRS HERRITON *writes a note*)

PHILIP. Italy in August would make *you* go barefoot, sister o'mine.

HARRIET. You may joke all you like, Philip, but *I* think it's tragic that an English baby should get such a terrible start in life.

PHILIP (*maliciously*) Passing over the point that it's an Italian baby, its start could hardly have been more edifying. You may be sure it was promptly christened at Santa Deodata's and is now watched over by a powerful combination of saints.

HARRIET. Call that a christening? A priest mumbling over it in a Papist church?

PHILIP. There's more beauty and sincerity in a single mass at Santa Deodata than in all the services ever performed by your chums at the Back Kitchen.

MRS HERRITON (*before Harriet can explode*) You really mustn't call Saint James's a "back kitchen", even in fun, Philip. (*She picks up her note and two library books from the desk and holds them out to Harriet*) Here are the names of the two new books I want. And, dear, when you discuss the baby with Irma, don't keep saying how much you pity it. Your feelings do you credit, but . . . (*She hesitates*)

(HARRIET *moves to Mrs Herriton and takes the books and the note*)

PHILIP. Mother means that if Irma suspects the father is a bad lot, she'll be frantic to get us to rescue it from him.

HARRIET (*sighing*) I must say I couldn't blame her. But I'll be careful what I say to her, Mother.

(IRMA *enters through the arch*)

IRMA. Miss Abbot to see you and Aunt Harriet, Grandmother.

(MRS HERRITON *gives the merest fleeting frown of dismay, then rises*)

MRS HERRITON (*calling graciously*) Caroline, my dear! Do come in. (*She moves to* L *of the armchair* RC)

(IRMA *stands aside above the arch.* HARRIET *moves above the armchair* L. PHILIP *goes to the bookcase, stubs out his cigarette in the ashtray on it, blows through his cigarette holder, puts it in his pocket and moves down* R.

CAROLINE ABBOTT *enters through the arch, smiles kindly at Irma as she passes her, and crosses to* C. CAROLINE *is a year or two younger than Philip, slender and extremely well-made, although her clothes do much to conceal the latter fact. Her features have an almost classic beauty, yet somehow few people think of her as beautiful. She looks kind, amiable, not unintelligent, and dull.* PHILIP *bows coldly.* CAROLINE *bows to Mrs Herriton then turns to* HARRIET *who greets her with sincere pleasure*)

HARRIET (*moving to Caroline*) Caroline, how nice! (*She pecks Caroline's cheek*) I was hoping we'd see you, before you deserted us for the Continent. You go tomorrow, don't you?

CAROLINE. Yes, very early. (*She turns and shakes hands with Mrs Herriton*) Good morning, Mrs Herriton. I wanted to say good-bye in case I should get too busy later in the day to do so. And to ask if there is anything you and Harriet would like me to buy for you while I'm abroad.

MRS HERRITON. How very kind and thoughtful of you, my dear. Let me see—(*she crosses below Caroline and Harriet to the work-table*) I have been wanting a very small piece of Chantilly lace—about sixteen inches—to trim . . .

IRMA (*breaking in eagerly and moving to* L *of Caroline*) Are you going abroad, Miss Abbott?

MRS HERRITON. Grandmother was speaking, dear.
IRMA (*crossing below Harriet to Mrs Herriton*) Excuse me for interrupting you, Grandmother. (*She bursts out again*) I just thought if Miss Abbott were going to Italy, she might take a present to my little brother for me.

(CAROLINE *starts and looks at Philip.* MRS HERRITON *compresses her lips*)

(*She continues, unaware of the others' reactions*) I wouldn't have time to make him the socks but I might buy him something, while Aunt Harriet and I are in the High Street. I saw an ever so sweet rattle, blue, with tiny bells . . .
MRS HERRITON. I'm afraid Miss Abbott cannot be your messenger, Irma. She's spending her holiday on the Normandy coast in France. That is a very long way from Italy.
IRMA (*disappointed*) Oh.
MRS HERRITON. You and Aunt Harriet had better run along now, dear, or you will get back late for your piano lesson.
HARRIET. Yes, Irma. (*She pushes Irma across to Caroline*) Say goodbye to Miss Abbott and come along.
IRMA (*to Caroline*) Good-bye. I hope you have a nice holiday.
CAROLINE (*smiling*) Thank you, Irma. I hope you get time to make those socks later and that they turn out well.
IRMA. Thank you.

(HARRIET *takes* IRMA'S *hand and leads her to the arch*)

HARRIET. We shan't be long, Caroline—do wait until we come back. (*She stops and turns*) I want to give you the address of a restaurant in Dieppe where one can get real English cooking.

(IRMA *and* HARRIET *exit through the arch*)

MRS HERRITON. Won't you sit down, Caroline? That is, if you can spare the time. I know how many things one has to do on the eve of a holiday. (*She sits in the armchair* L)

(PHILIP *moves behind the armchair* RC)

CAROLINE (*crossing to the armchair* RC) Thank you. (*She sits*) Irma seems very happy about her baby brother. I am glad you decided to tell her, at last.
PHILIP (*moving down* R; *brusquely*) The decision was thrust upon us. Carella sent her a postcard that gave the show away. (*He indicates the pieces of card on the table* RC)
CAROLINE (*glancing at the pieces of postcard*) Oh, I see. (*She looks thoughtfully at Mrs Herriton for a few moments*)

(MRS HERRITON *appears slightly uncomfortable*)

(*To Mrs Herriton*) Still, she knows. That quite alters the situation, doesn't it?

PHILIP. Not in the least. The child is no relation of ours. We can do nothing for it.

MRS HERRITON (*glancing nervously at Philip*) I know what Caroline means. Poor Lillia had no close relations of her own. She looked on us as her real family rather than in-laws. (*To Caroline*) I had intended to tell you before you went away, my dear; the estate is finally settled and my solicitors have written me all the details, as I requested.

CAROLINE (*politely*) Yes?

MRS HERRITON. The income Lillia had from what Charles left her in trust reverts to Irma. But her own money she left to Carella. It's not a large sum but it will take care of the child's needs—especially in Italy where everything is so much cheaper.

CAROLINE. I don't think money alone can take care of his needs. It is a question of upbringing.

PHILIP. You have so many other good works to occupy you, Miss Abbott, that it's amazingly kind of you to take an interest in this baby.

CAROLINE. He would not have come into the world if I had acted differently. Naturally I take an interest.

MRS HERRITON. My dear Caroline, we forgave you long ago for your part in that unfortunate marriage. Let bygones be bygones.

CAROLINE. You may have forgiven me, but I can't forgive myself. (*She turns to Philip as though she really wanted him to understand her attitude*) Lillia relied a great deal on my judgement. The man she married has turned out dissolute and cruel. He made her suffer so terribly that she was probably glad to die. And I encouraged the match in every way I could.

PHILIP (*in a gentler tone*) But, Miss Abbott, you're blowing up the whole affair into a Renaissance tragedy. Carella is no Cesare Borgia. He's a vulgar young cad with black glossy hair and teeth almost as white as the ones his father makes. As for Lillia—well, with all due respect for the dead, she was hardly the stuff from which tragic heroines are made.

CAROLINE (*quietly*) You mean, because she was shallow and rather silly? Do you think only profound, intellectual people can suffer?

PHILIP. The point I was trying to make . . .

CAROLINE. I know. You think I am making too much fuss about a mistake in judgement. But I did something far worse: I failed Lillia twice again—out of sheer cowardice. The first time was when we got your telegram saying you were coming to Monteriano. I knew you were coming to try and stop the marriage . . .

PHILIP. Which had already taken place. (*He still resents this and shows it*)

CAROLINE. Yes. I was sure you would be angry. So I ran away in a panic and let Lillia to face you alone.

PHILIP (*acidly*) Alone! Not at all. She had her new husband. I assure you they both felt nothing but hilarity at my charge across Europe to prevent a *fait accompli*.

CAROLINE. That doesn't excuse me for running away. The second time I behaved like a coward was when she wrote to me. Or rather, simply poured all her despair on to paper and sent it to me, because there was no-one else who cared a straw.

PHILIP. Mother told me about that letter, Miss Abbott. I can see how it distressed you.

MRS HERRITON. It distressed us all. I couldn't sleep for nights after you showed it to Harriet and me.

CAROLINE. That was my chance to make Lillia some compensation. I could have gone and stayed with her until her child was born. At the very least it would have relieved her loneliness and her fear of him. But I did nothing.

MRS HERRITON. Come, my dear! You answered her letter at once and . . .

CAROLINE. Oh, yes. I wrote sensible advice about not giving way to despair. And made cheerful predictions that the baby would make her marriage work better—not one word of which I believed myself. (*She resumes the even, colourless tone she has used earlier*) Well, the only compensation I can make her now is to see that her child is brought up by people with decent standards and some sense of responsibility.

MRS HERRITON (*rising and moving down* C) After you have come back from your holiday, we will try to work out a plan together.

(PHILIP *moves above the armchair* RC)

CAROLINE. I have had a plan for some time, Mrs Herriton. And now I feel free to act on it. I am going to adopt the child myself.

(*This calm, almost casually uttered statement affects* MRS HERRITON *rather more than if Caroline had hurled a grenade in her face.* PHILIP *is astonished, but less disagreeably so*)

PHILIP. You can't be serious.

CAROLINE. Indeed I am. Of course I wouldn't presume to take him if Mrs Herriton wanted him, but since she doesn't . . . (*She rises and moves to* R *of Mrs Herriton*) As I said, I have been considering it for some time. I thought there was no point in discussing it with you while you were still opposed to telling Irma about the baby's existence. But she has found out so there is nothing to prevent me from making my offer to Signor Carella immediately.

MRS HERRITON (*sharply*) Nonsense! You can't do this thing, Caroline.

CAROLINE. I see no reason why not, Mrs Herriton.

MRS HERRITON. There are a hundred reasons! There's—there's your father. How do you think he will like to be burdened, at his age, with all the trouble and expense of rearing a child?

CAROLINE. I shall look after the child myself, and pay for his schooling and all the other expenses out of my own money.

PHILIP. I hope you're including Signor Carella's selling price

B

among your expenses. If you want the baby posted by return you'd better include a good round sum in your letter.

CAROLINE. Thank you for your advice, Mr Herriton, but I don't think Signor Carella is the kind of man to be dealt with by letter. (*She holds out her hand*) Good-bye, Mrs Herriton.

(MRS HERRITON *takes Caroline's hand briefly*)

I'll drop you a line as soon as Signor Carella and I have reached an agreement. (*She turns to Philip*) Good-bye, Mr Herriton. (*She crosses to the arch*)

PHILIP (*crossing to the arch*) I'll see you out.

(CAROLINE *exits through the arch.*

PHILIP *pauses a moment, glances at Mrs Herriton, then follows Caroline off. At once a startling change comes over* MRS HERRITON. *Her face grows red and congested. She paces back and forth, goes up* RC *to the desk, suddenly strikes it with a clenched fist, and mutters under her breath.*

PHILIP *re-enters through the arch*)

(*He moves* LC) Well, I said she was barmy, but I understated it.

MRS HERRITON (*moving down* C; *in the thick voice of frustrated rage*) The impudence of her—the damned impudence!

PHILIP (*staring at her; astonished*) Mother!

MRS HERRITON. Yes, I'm cursing and I don't care! How dare she disgrace me!

PHILIP. What do you mean, Mother? Disgrace you to whom?

MRS HERRITON. To everyone in Sawston! The sanctimonious, meddling . . . (*She breaks off and sways*)

(PHILIP *moves quickly to* MRS HERRITON, *takes her arm and leads her to the armchair* RC)

PHILIP (*with an undertone of distaste*) Do sit down, Mother. You'll have another heart attack.

(MRS HERRITON *sits in the armchair* RC *and struggles to compose herself.* PHILIP *stands* L *of her*)

MRS HERRITON. I'm sorry, Philip. But can't you see how it will look for my daughter-in-law's child—my grand-daughter's brother—to be brought up almost at our gates, by a person—a young woman who has no connection with him at all?

PHILIP (*crossing down* L) What could be a neater solution? Irma can see her darling brother as often as she pleases; we get peace from Irma—and all the trouble and cost are borne by someone else.

MRS HERRITON. You are shockingly cynical. It is the very last outcome I should wish. She'll go around telling everyone that she rescued the baby from a wicked father who would have ruined its life. And people will either say we grudged the money or that we are callous and irresponsible for not having rescued it ourselves.

PHILIP. If anyone is ass enough to think we have the slightest responsibility to that blasted brat . . .

Mrs Herriton. Whatever they *think*, you may be sure that's what they'll say.

Philip. Then let them say it. Who cares?

Mrs Herriton. I do. I have never been a laughing-stock or an object of censure, and I don't intend to become one now. (*She rises and crosses to* R *of Philip*) Philip, dear, you don't understand how malicious people are—how they welcome the chance to undermine anyone of a certain position and standing. And that wretched Caroline Abbott may go straight to Italy and get the baby if we don't stop her.

Philip. Not "we", Mother. I tried to stop Lillia's marriage for you and only made a fool of myself. (*He moves to the armchair* L *and sits*) This time it's entirely your affair.

(Mrs Herriton *glances at* Philip's *cold face and sees he means what he says*)

Mrs Herriton (*turning away* RC) Of course, dear. I realize that. Very well. (*She moves up* C)

Philip. Mother, you let Harriet be Low Church and dream of becoming a missionary. You let me study architecture and dream of tearing Sawston down and rebuilding it as a place of beauty. Let Caroline Abbott go to Monteriano and dream of returning with the baby. Let her mess with Italy by herself—if she has the temerity. She'll come to grief, believe me. Carella will marry her or murder her or do for her somehow.

Mrs Herriton (*moving down* LC) What rubbish! You've said repeatedly that he's only a common little . . .

Philip. I know. He's a bounder, but he isn't an English bounder. He's subtle and dangerous. And he's got a country behind him that's the same—a country that has upset people from the beginning of time.

Mrs Herriton (*looking thoughtfully at Philip*) You haven't been to Italy for quite a while, have you, dear? I expect you miss it.

Philip. Sometimes. It's a place that gets under one's skin, rather, and . . . (*He breaks off and eyes Mrs Herriton suspiciously*) What are you up to?

Mrs Herriton. Up to? I asked if you were still fond of Italy because you were going on about it upsetting people and so forth. (*She moves to the desk chair and sits*)

Philip. I see.

Mrs Herriton. In any case, let's keep Caroline Abbott's scheme between you and me for the time being.

(*The sound of scales and five-finger exercises being played rather thumpingly on a piano, is heard off* L)

Philip. If you like. (*He glances at his watch and rises*) Well, I must be off. I may have no clients, but I have got an office and if I'm not in it by ten o'clock, Sawston will call me a wastrel.

Mrs Herriton. The clients will come, Philip.

(HARRIET *enters through the arch, carrying two library books.*
PHILIP, *without replying to Mrs Herriton, brushes past Harriet, with a brief nod, and exits through the arch*)

HARRIET (*moving to* L *of Mrs Herriton*) Both the books you wanted were in, Mother. (*She puts the books on the desk*)
MRS HERRITON. Good. (*She listens approvingly to the piano*) And you got Irma back in time for her piano lesson.
HARRIET (*nodding*) She began to tell Miss Maynard straight off, about the baby. I didn't know whether I should try to stop her.
MRS HERRITON. Why should she be stopped? Dear child, she has seen this thing more clearly than any of us. She longs for her little brother. Have we the right to deprive her of him?

(*The piano playing ceases*)

HARRIET (*confused*) But—Mother—you said before she'd be just as happy if we bought her a puppy or some baby rabbits.
MRS HERRITON (*with a change of tactics*) Well—er—there is another aspect—a far more important one, that *you* have made me see, Harriet.
HARRIET (*flattered*) Really? Which one?
MRS HERRITON. Our moral responsibility to the baby himself. Ought he to be left in that place and with that father? With a man who will bring him up as a Papist or an infidel—who is certain, in any case, to bring him up immoral?

(*The piano exercises recommence*)

HARRIET (*her face lighting up*) Oh, Mother! I am so glad you've come to feel that, too.
MRS HERRITON. I feel it so strongly that I've decided to make the father an offer of adoption.
HARRIET. Oh, Mother, I do think you're wonderful.

(*An especially dull Czerny exercise is played on the piano*)

MRS HERRITON. I don't care if I am impulsive. (*With a considering air*) No! I'm not sure it's wise to write at all. No, I think a person of his type is best dealt with directly. How soon do you think you can be ready to go to Italy?
HARRIET. I? You want me to go and see that horrible man? (*She girds herself, like an early Christian who has caught the first whiff of the lions*) Very well, if you think that's the best way. He speaks some English, doesn't he?
MRS HERRITON. Quite a bit, I believe. But you need not even meet him. Your brother will conduct the negotiations. Your task will be to see that Philip doesn't give up if there should be difficulties. He hasn't your determination, Harriet. And his weakness for Italy and Italians is another thing that makes me uneasy about him. I want that baby and I want it immediately—and since Dr Stevens won't let me travel, I count on you to get it for me.

(*The piano playing ceases*)

HARRIET (*with dedicated fervour*) Rest assured, Mother. I won't come back without it.

MRS HERRITON (*rising and laying a hand on Harriet's shoulder*) You are a great comfort to me, my dear. (*She crosses to the bookcase* R, *takes out a copy of "Bradshaw", moves above the armchair* RC *to* L *of it and turns the pages of the time-table*)

HARRIET (*glowing with happiness*) Thank you, Mother. I do try to be. I think I'll run across the road and tell Caroline Abbot about this. She takes almost as keen an interest in the poor baby as we do and she'll be so happy to hear that . . .

MRS HERRITON. I'll tell Caroline myself, dear. I should like the pleasure of seeing her happiness when she learns that we are taking the child into our own home. Now, I just want to look up the boat-trains and then I shall go straight over. You had better begin sorting out your things and decide what you will need for the journey.

HARRIET. I expect I should. Oh, it's fine to think that out of all the evil of Lillia's marriage, good will come at last. (*She moves to the arch*)

MRS HERRITON. Yes, isn't it? Oh, by the way, Harriet.

(HARRIET *stops and turns*)

Don't say anything to Philip just yet about going to Italy. He might not like our making plans without consulting him. He's quite touchy, you know.

HARRIET (*her happiness increased by this conspiracy against her brother*) Ridiculously so. I understand, Mother.

MRS HERRITON. Not a word until I've talked to him first. He requires very tactful handling.

(IRMA's *piano lesson becomes much more audible. She has advanced from Czerny to a simple, merry little country dance, Schumann's "Merry Peasant". She plays it very badly but loudly and enthusiastically*)

HARRIET. Not a word.

(HARRIET *exits through the arch.* MRS HERRITON *listens to the piano for a moment, frowns slightly and crosses to the arch*)

MRS HERRITON (*calling in a clear, carrying voice*) Miss Maynard! Miss Maynard!

(*The piano playing ceases*)

I don't think Irma is advanced enough yet for tunes. She had better stick to exercises.

MRS HERRITON *consults the "Bradshaw", finds the train she seeks, turns down the corner of the page, crosses and returns the time-table to the bookcase. The supremely dreary Czerny exercise is resumed on the piano.* MRS HERRITON *notices the pieces of postcard on the table* RC *and gathers them up in her hand. Standing erect, she suddenly tosses the collection of* torn pieces into the air a little way and catches them with the same hand. It is a fleeting gesture but it expresses satisfaction as eloquently as a triumphant grin. She then moves to the desk, lets the scraps of card flutter into the waste-paper basket, picks up her hat, puts it on and exits through the arch as—

the LIGHTS *dim to* BLACK-OUT

The Czerny exercise continues and during the scene change, cross fades to a recording of Caruso singing "O Paradiso" from "L'Africaine", by Meyerbeer. This continues when Scene 2 commences.

SCENE 2

SCENE—*The salone of the Hotel Stella d'Italia, Monteriano, Italy. A week later. About 10 p.m.*
The Stella d'Italia was a ducal palace in the fifteenth century and traces of its former splendour remain in the windows L, *with their delicately carved mouldings. These windows, which evoke the Renaissance, look out on a survival of the Middle Ages. The Cappochi Tower. Wedged between mean houses, it rises massive and noble from a base covered with advertisements to a summit radiant in the sun, or luminous and unearthly in moonlight. Otherwise, this is unmistakably an Italian hotel of the second class: one of those places that the guide-books describes as "Clean—Modest Comforts". The décor is a mixture of styles, periods and colours, with a leaning towards lurid pinks and swaggering greens. The hotel's opposite number in England or America would be dreary or squalid, but there is a cheerful ease about this place that saves it from being either. The entrance to the street is down* L. *A curtained doorway up* RC *leads into the dining-room and kitchen quarters. A curved staircase up* L *leads up and off* C *to the bedrooms. The reception desk is* R. *Some of the furniture is shabby and old, a few pieces so new you can see your face in the varnish. A marble-topped table stands* C *with a rush-seated armchair* R *of it and a rush-seated upright chair* L *of it. There is an upright chair down* R, *a small stool-table* L *of the door up* RC, *and a small stool above the entrance down* L. *There is a rack of clothes hooks over the stool up* RC. *Behind the reception desk there is a key-rack with keys; a clock high up on the wall; a letter-rack with letters in it; a calendar and a coloured picture of Victor Emmanuel, in a red velvet frame. On the wall up* C, *there is a picture of Santa Deodata, in a gold frame, and on the staircase wall, a gold-framed picture of the towers and hills as on the postcard in Scene 1. A double gas bracket, with chains, over the picture of Santa Deodata, furnishes most of the illumination at night. There is also a single gas bracket on the wall behind the desk and an oil lamp on a ledge halfway up the stairs.*
When the LIGHTS *come up, the light fittings are on and the window shutters are closed. Music is pouring from the horn of an old-fashioned gramophone on the reception desk. The music is of Caruso singing "O Paradiso" from*

To face page 16—Where Angels Fear to Tread

Photograph by Angus McBean

SCENE 2   WHERE ANGELS FEAR TO TREAD

"*L'Africaine*" *by Meyerbeer.* SIGNORA ALETTI, *the proprietress, is behind the desk, watering a pot of begonias on it. She seems too intent on her task to be listening to Caruso, but when he reaches his climatic passage, she looks up attentively, gives a beaming nod, blows a kiss to the gramophone, then gives a satisfied sigh. She pours the remaining drops of water from the jug on to the plant, then stops the gramophone. She puts down the jug, yawns, glances at the clock and crosses to the armchair* R *of the table* C. *She picks up a fan from the chair, fans herself, puts the fan on the table* C, *moves up* C, *kisses the picture of Santa Deodata, then pulls the chain of the gas bracket and dims the light, leaving the small light behind the desk and the oil lamp on the stairs. With another yawn she exits up the stairs. There is a short pause then* PHILIP *enters down* L. *His left arm is in a sling and he looks tired, hot and irritable. He crosses to the desk, puts his hat on it, moves* C, *glances around, then moves down* L.

PHILIP (*calling*) Come in, Harriet, come in. The cab driver can bring the luggage without your supervision.

HARRIET (*off* L; *calling*) What's to prevent his making off with it, if there's no-one to watch him?

(PHILIP *makes an annoyed sound and sinks wearily on to the chair* L *of the table* C.

HARRIET *enters down* L. *She is wearing a thin, dark travelling dress and the same hat as in Scene I. She has got a speck of grit in her eye and is trying to extract it with her handkerchief*)

Not that I can watch much with this eye. Oh, dear, whatever can have got in it?

PHILIP. A cobblestone, probably. I fall out of railway carriages and break my bones. Foreign matter of every description flies into your eyes. We lose tickets and leave things behind in hotels.

(HARRIET *crosses to the desk*)

Obviously, St Christopher draws the line at looking after fools who will travel in August. (*He mops his perspiring face*)

(*The* CAB DRIVER *enters down* L. *He carries two suitcases, one with a lady's umbrella strapped to it, and a lady's red dressing-case. He puts the cases on the floor down* L)

HARRIET. Where's the manageress or the hall porter or whoever's supposed to receive us? (*She strikes the handbell on the desk, commandingly, but it remains mute*)

CAB DRIVER. Non va, signorina. Rotto.

(HARRIET *again strikes the bell*)

PHILIP. It's broken.

CAB DRIVER (*to Philip*) Scusate, signore—la luce.

(PHILIP *rises, crosses below the table and sits in the chair* R *of it*)

(*He moves* L *of the table to the gas bracket up* C, *pulls the chain and brings up the light. With a sweeping hospitable gesture*) Si accomodi! Vado a cecare la padrona. (*He moves to the door up* RC *and calls*) Signora Aletti!

(*The* CAB DRIVER *exits up* RC. HARRIET *finally gets the speck from her eye, crosses to the foot of the stairs and examines the salone with disfavour*)

HARRIET. This doesn't look much of a place, I must say.

PHILIP. I found it comfortable enough the last time and the food is very good.

HARRIET (*moving* L) No Italian food is good. (*She gives a martyr's sigh*) Well, we aren't here for pleasure. From what I saw of Monteriano from the carriage, I can't imagine anyone coming here if they didn't have to do so.

PHILIP. Dear Harriet! What a help your sweetness and tact will be when we talk to Carella.

HARRIET. Nothing would induce me to speak to that man.

PHILIP. Then why the devil did you come? For ornament?

HARRIET (*moving down* L *of the table*) To see that you do your duty. Mother was afraid you might neglect it if you came alone.

(*The* CAB DRIVER *enters up* C, *preventing a savage retort from* PHILIP)

CAB DRIVER (*crossing to the luggage*) La Padrona deve essere sopra. Prenderò i bagagli sù, e la troverò. (*He picks up the luggage and moves to the stairs*)

(HARRIET *snatches the dressing-case from the Cab Driver and puts it on the chair* L *of the table*)

PHILIP. *Tante grazie.*

CAB DRIVER. Prego.

(*The* CAB DRIVER *exits up the stairs*)

PHILIP (*to Harriet; angrily*) So mother told you I wasn't to be trusted alone, did she?

HARRIET. She did. (*She speaks without shrillness, but with a sincere indignation attaining one of the rare moments when it is impossible not to respect her*) And I can certainly understand her fears. You think I'm a fool, Philip, because I don't go in for cleverness. But I have been noticing you all today and you have talked about churches and pictures and scenery and history—everything but the baby. You haven't thought of it once. You haven't planned what you will say to Carella. You don't care!

PHILIP. I'll go and see him tomorrow.

(*The* CAB DRIVER *enters down the stairs*)

CAB DRIVER (*moving to* L *of Harriet*) Complimenti della Signora Aletti—lei viene giù in un momento.

PHILIP (*taking some coins from his pocket*) Bene.

HARRIET. What's he say?
PHILIP. He says the signora will be down in a minute. (*He holds the coins out to the Cab Driver*) Ecco!
CAB DRIVER (*crossing below Harriet to Philip*) Molte grazie, signore. (*He takes the coins*)
PHILIP. Prego. Arrivederci!
CAB DRIVER. Arrivederci! (*He crosses below Harriet to* L, *benevolently including her in his wish*) E la signorina—arrivederci! Buona permanenza a Monteriano.

(*The* CAB DRIVER *exits down* L)

HARRIET (*resuming her indictment of Philip*) And now you're postponing the interview. You promised mother faithfully you wouldn't delay—and look at you now. Loafing about. You simply don't care.
PHILIP. Harriet, it is hot. (*He picks up the fan from the table and fans himself*) Also I am tired and my arm hurts. I care about nothing, at present, but a cool drink and bed.
HARRIET (*snatching the fan from Philip; her temper flaring*) You'll get neither until you've talked to Carella. Go and see him now. This instant.
PHILIP. I'm blowed if I will.

(SIGNORA ALETTI *enters on the stairs*)

SIGNORA ALETTI. Buona sera.

(PHILIP *rises, moves a step downstage and turns to Signora Aletti.* HARRIET *turns and crosses to* L *of the stairs*)

PHILIP. Buona sera, signora.
SIGNORA ALETTI (*to Philip; welcome and apology equally fervent*) Ah—Signore Herriton—benvenuto. Mi dispiace infinitamente averla fatta aspettare.
PHILIP. Non fa niente, signora. Vorrei due camere—per favore.

(SIGNORA ALETTI *starts to come down the stairs.* HARRIET *goes up to the second stair, stops and turns her back to Signora Aletti*)

You're in the way, Harriet.

(HARRIET *does not budge*)

Harriet, let the signora come down.
HARRIET. No.
PHILIP (*crossing to* L *of the stairs*) Then let me go up with her and choose our rooms.
HARRIET. *No!*
PHILIP. Are you mad?
HARRIET. If you like. But you shan't go up until you've seen Carella.

(PHILIP *makes a move to pass* HARRIET, *who instantly stretches out her arms to bar him, one hand flat against the wall, the other gripping the rail)*

PHILIP *(to the signora)* La signorina e malata—fa troppo caldo per lei.
SIGNORA ALETTI. Poveretta! Il tempo fa brutto. *(She leans solicitously over Harriet's shoulder)* Soffre di vertigini, signorina? *(In laborious English)* The heat give you dizziness? *(She puts a hand on Harriet's shoulder)*
HARRIET *(snapping)* No! *(She throws off the signora's hand)* Leave me alone. *(To Philip)* Telling her lies about me won't do you any good. Mother expects us to get that baby *quickly*. I shan't budge until I see you go out of that door. *(Her voice rising)* I won't let you dawdle and postpone and . . .

(SIGNORA ALETTI glances anxiously up the stairs and puts a finger to her lips)

SIGNORA ALETTI. Lo prego. Piano—piano.
PHILIP *(crossing down* R*)* In heaven's name, be quiet, Harriet! Haven't you the very slightest sense of the ludicrous?
SIGNORA ALETTI. Scusi tante, Signorina Abbott.

(CAROLINE enters at the top of the stairs and looks down at them. PHILIP stares at her with astonishment, and wrath. He has been manipulated by his mother, hectored and shamed by his sister. The intervention of a third female is the last straw)

PHILIP *(slowly and savagely)* Well, I'm damned! This is the last straw!

(HARRIET turns and sees Caroline)

HARRIET *(with a shrill cry of pleased surprise)* Caroline! You here, of all people. *(She forgets her barricade of the stairs and moves down them to* L *of the table* C*)*

(SIGNORA ALETTI takes advantage of the distraction to come down the stairs and cross to the desk. PHILIP *deliberately turns his back on Caroline and addresses the signora.* CAROLINE *comes down the stairs)*

PHILIP. *Favarisca, datemi vino bianco. Molto freddo.*

(CAROLINE and HARRIET exchange kisses on the cheek and are talking, HARRIET *eagerly.* CAROLINE *reserved and ill at ease)*

SIGNORA ALETTI. Con piacere, Signore.

(SIGNORA ALETTI picks up the water jug from the desk and exits up RC. PHILIP *moves to the desk, picks up a magazine, then sits in the chair down* R *and reads)*

HARRIET *(to Caroline)* I thought you were in Normandy. How long have you been here?
CAROLINE. I only arrived yesterday.
HARRIET *(fanning herself)* We were supposed to arrive yesterday,

too. But Philip slipped getting off the train at Florence and broke his arm. (*She sounds as though he had done this to show off*) He fell right on it. So we had to stop the night. Oh, it's been a dreadful trip. I lost my hot-water bottle at the hotel in Paris—brand new and of course I'll never get it back.

CAROLINE (*crossing below Harriet to* C) I'm sorry about your accident, Mr Herriton. I hope you were able to get the arm set properly.

HARRIET. Oh, yes. The doctor was English. Recommended by the consul. (*She dismisses Philip's arm*) Caroline, I think it's perfectly splendid of you to come to this awful place to help us.

(PHILIP *glances up and smiles unpleasantly.* CAROLINE *looks uncomfortable.*

SIGNORA ALETTI *enters up* C *carrying a tray with a carafe of wine and a glass. She puts the tray on the stool-table up* RC, *moves it to Philip and pours a glass of wine*)

Now, don't deny that's why you're here. Mother told me that you felt just as strongly as we do that the poor baby must be rescued.

CAROLINE. Yes, I do feel very strongly about that.

HARRIET. And you know Carella. That makes you an invaluable ally. I wish you'd advise us on the best tone to take with him. Philip is going to see him in a minute.

SIGNORA ALETTI (*handing the glass to Philip*) Eccolo, Signore. Freddo come la neve.

(PHILIP *sips the wine*)

HARRIET (*her brow darkening*) Philip!

PHILIP. 'Squisito, Signora.

HARRIET (*throwing the fan on to the table*) Philip!

(SIGNORA ALETTI *bows to Philip, goes behind the desk, consults her ledger then takes two keys from the key rack*)

CAROLINE. Mr Herriton won't find Signor Carella at his house now, Harriet. Signor Carella spends the evenings with his friends at a café in the piazza. He never gets home before midnight.

PHILIP (*to Harriet*) It would hardly do to interview him in a public place, surrounded by his cronies.

HARRIET. I suppose not. Very well, then you may wait until tomorrow morning. (*To Caroline*) You see, Caroline, you've already been helpful. You know the creature's habits and we don't.

(SIGNORA ALETTI *moves with the keys to Philip*)

CAROLINE (*stiffly*) I know how he used to spend his evenings, from what Lillia said in her letter. I assume he hasn't changed.

PHILIP. You look thoroughly tired out, Harriet. Why don't you go up and choose the rooms and settle in?

HARRIET (*picking up her dressing-case*) Well, I should like to get out my spirit lamp and make myself some tea.

PHILIP (*to the Signora*) Signora vuol faccia vedere le camere a mia sorella.

SIGNORA ALETTI. Con piacere. (*She crosses below the others to the stairs and smiles benevolently at Harriet*) Come with me, please, mees.

PHILIP (*pointedly*) Perhaps Miss Abbot will help you unpack.

CAROLINE. I should like to talk to you first, Mr Herriton.

HARRIET. Yes, do. Tell him the best way to deal with Carella. I'm sure you'll save him from making mistakes.

(SIGNORA ALETTI *exits up the stairs.*

HARRIET *follows her off.* CAROLINE *moves to the armchair* R *of the table nearer to Philip, and sits*)

CAROLINE. I realize you'd rather be left alone, Mr Herriton, but there isn't time.

PHILIP (*with a lift of his eyebrows*) Really? (*He rises and moves up* RC) Will you have some wine? I know where the *padrona* keeps the glasses.

CAROLINE. No, thank you. Harriet will be with you in the morning and we can't speak frankly before her. I think we can to one another and that we should do so. Otherwise we'll never start clear.

PHILIP. By all means let us start clear. (*He moves to the table* C *and throws his magazine on it*) I'll begin by asking you a question. (*He moves* C *and turns to Caroline*) In which role are you really here: ally or rival?

CAROLINE. Neither. Spy.

(PHILIP *looks at her, surprised by the coolness of this admission*)

(*Crisply*) I don't trust your mother. She never wanted the child. No harm in that if she'd said so at the beginning. But she didn't. She put me off with evasions—some clever, some nonsensical. She has told Harriet nothing. She has behaved dishonestly all through.

PHILIP (*discomfited*) I won't deny that mother didn't want the child at first. However, she came to feel differently and I understand she told you so. It's also my understanding that you were pleased and satisfied with her decision.

CAROLINE. I pretended to be. In Sawston one has to pretend about most things. But I knew Mrs Herriton didn't feel differently about the child. She only wanted to prevent me from adopting it— for the sake of appearances.

PHILIP. But, Miss Abbott . . .

CAROLINE. Don't let's argue. If you are here to get the child, I will help you. If you are here to make a gesture and fail, I shall get it for myself.

PHILIP (*crossing to the wine and refilling his glass*) I give you my word that we're not here to fail. Mother has fixed no money limit whatsoever on what we're to give Carella. She is as determined now to have the child as she formerly was to avoid taking it. You may find that hard to believe.

CAROLINE (*nodding*) Not at all. She is still exercising power. The object is reversed, but for Mrs Herriton the object has always been secondary to the power itself. Yes, I believe you.

PHILIP (*reverting to his dry, satirical manner*) Thank you. You understand then that Harriet and I are here to carry out mother's instructions, and you approve the instructions?

(CAROLINE *nods*)

You should, since you have virtually dictated them. I think they're completely absurd, but no matter.

CAROLINE (*rising*) Why did you come, if you feel like that?

PHILIP. I can't resist a comic spectacle, and this rescue party is a sort of Guignol with the puppets working each other. Mother worked by you; Harriet worked by mother; Carella worked by Harriet and me—or more exactly, by the money in our pockets.

(CAROLINE *makes no comment and turns away* LC)

(*After a pause*) I can guess what you're thinking. All right, I'm a puppet's puppet, too—but at least I know the exact disposition of the strings. (*He pauses and moves* C) I think you'd better take charge, Miss Abbott. As Harriet says, you know Carella's ways and we don't.

CAROLINE (*moving* L) I saw him yesterday—quite by chance. He thought I was here as a tourist and I let him think so. (*She frowns slightly*) He was very civil. He invited me to come and see the baby.

PHILIP. Splendid! I think it would be a good idea for you to accept his invitation tomorrow morning. Alone.

CAROLINE (*indignantly*) Mr Herriton! Do you think I would go alone to that man's house, knowing about him all I do? You have very odd ideas about what's possible for a lady.

(PHILIP *smiles*)

Why are you smiling?

PHILIP. Because I see there are two Miss Abbotts. One who can travel all the way to Monteriano alone in order to rescue a baby from Carella—and another who can't enter Carella's house when she gets here.

CAROLINE (*suddenly smiling*) I suppose it *is* foolish. Do you want me to go there first and more or less pave the way for you?

PHILIP. Exactly. Explain to him why we've come, in a tactful, general way. I'll follow in about half an hour and make him a definite offer. You see, he has some reason to resent me. I made no bones about what I thought of Lillia marrying him. You, on the contrary, he must think of as an ally.

CAROLINE (*moving to the window down* L *and pushing the shutter open*) Yes, I know . . . There's a breeze springing up. (*She gazes out of the window for a moment then gives an impulsive cry of delight*) Just look at that tower in the moonlight.

(PHILIP *crosses to the stairs and leans against the newel post. He and* CAROLINE *both look out at the Cappochi Tower silvered with the light of a crescent moon which its summit seems to touch*)

PHILIP. Its summit in heaven, its base plastered with advertisements for hair-oil. It might be a symbol of Italy.

CAROLINE. When I was here with Lillia, I only noticed the heavenly part. No, that's not true. It was very much of the earth, but—but an earth I hadn't known existed.

PHILIP (*nodding understandingly*) Because it *doesn't* exist at home—we won't allow it to. Its naturalness shocks us; we are frightened by its vigour; its gaiety is so simple that we call it childish.

CAROLINE. That is what I thought. I hated Sawston then, you see. (*She turns from the window*)

PHILIP (*delighted*) So did I. So *do* I. Go on.

CAROLINE. I hated the pretending, the respectability, the dullness, the petty unselfishness.

PHILIP. Petty *self*ishness.

CAROLINE (*shaking her head*) No! No! Petty *un*selfishness. Everyone making little sacrifices for things they don't care for, to please people they don't love. And I thought they had never learned much about loving anybody, for that matter.

PHILIP. Why, Miss Abbott! I had no idea you felt like this. You always seemed so ... (*He checks himself*) It's superb! I agree with every word of it.

CAROLINE. I am telling you what I thought eighteen months ago. (*She crosses below Philip to* C)

(PHILIP *moves down* L *of the table* C)

All that spring I seemed to be waking up to beauty and splendour and to the things that are more important even than wonderful sights like the Cappochi Tower there—gaiety, vigour, naturalness. That is why I misjudged Signor Carella: he had all three qualities —in abundance—so I imagined he was also sincere and kind. And Lillia—well, there were things I didn't like about her but she had somehow kept her power of enjoying life. I thought if they wanted to marry, why shouldn't they?

PHILIP. Did you never think of the disparity of their backgrounds?

CAROLINE (*moving to* R *of Philip*) I was drunk with rebellion. All that mattered was that she should escape from her deadening existence at home—from being lectured by your mother, bullied by Harriet and patronized by you. (*She gives him an apologetic look*) I'm sorry. That was rude.

PHILIP (*crossing below Caroline to the wine*) Am I truly so disagreeable? (*He refills his glass*)

CAROLINE (*turning to him*) No, Mr Herriton. If you were truly disagreeable you would have made enemies. But though you may hate Sawston, Sawston doesn't hate you. Oh, you're considered unconventional but no-one really minds. Some people say you're sarcastic, but they always add: "His bark is worse than his bite."

PHILIP (*with a slightly uncomfortable laugh*) I dare say that'll be my epitaph. Not a precisely glorious one but it could be worse.

(CAROLINE *is silent*)

You don't agree, do you? You'd rather see me sink my teeth in Sawston's throat?

CAROLINE. It would probably change nothing. (*She sits* L *of the table* C) Insensibility and spitefulness and mediocrity are invincible; if we try to go against them they will break us to pieces. I didn't know that when I urged Lillia to rebel—and look at the outcome. I only made her change one sort of groove for another—a far worse one. (*With an abrupt change to indignation*) Do you know that man actually spoke about her yesterday as though he mourned her? He pretended he had loved her. He was perfectly disgusting. He even offered to show me her grave.

(PHILIP *smiles at* CAROLINE'S *animation, which is very becoming*)

PHILIP. All Italians are essentially dramatic, Miss Abbott, and what drama is greater than death? I detest the fellow but I don't doubt, at the moment he talked to you, he honestly believed he was a grief-stricken widower who had always behaved admirably to his wife. (*He sits on the arm of the armchair* R *of the table*)

CAROLINE. Then I can only hope he has thousands of other moments when he remembers the truth and his conscience tortures him.

PHILIP. I'm afraid that's not likely. He was unfaithful to her but infidelity isn't the serious thing with Italians that it is with us. As I told Harriet, if you condemn him for that, you'll have to condemn nearly every married man in Italy. (*He drains his glass*)

CAROLINE. And what did Harriet say?

PHILIP (*rising and putting his glass on the table* R) She condemned the lot—and threw in the French for good measure.

CAROLINE (*with feeling*) I wish I were Harriet.

PHILIP. So do I occasionally. But if things were that simple they'd be terribly dull. (*He crosses below Caroline to* L. *With a contented sigh*) I say, that breeze has cooled things off wonderfully.

CAROLINE. Signor Carella said the heat would break tonight.

PHILIP. What else did you talk about?

CAROLINE. Oh, well—our whole conversation didn't last more than a few minutes. He asked if I found his English had improved. It has—greatly. That's Lillia's work. She never could learn Italian. (*She rises and moves* LC) I ran into him when I was coming down from the Rocca. You know—that broken tower on the top of a hill, where you can stand and see all the other towers and the plains and all the other hills.

PHILIP. Yes, I know. (*He quotes, affectionately*) "The view from the Rocca—small gratuity to gatekeeper—is finest at sunset." I say—

shall we prove *Baedeker* wrong? (*He moves to* L *of Caroline*) I'm sure it's every bit as fine by moonlight.

CAROLINE (*her face lighting with pleasure*) But aren't you too tired?

PHILIP (*crossing to the desk*) No—not any more. (*He picks up his hat*)

(CAROLINE *moves below the table* C.
HARRIET *enters on the stairs*)

HARRIET (*calling*) Philip! Are you coming up, now?

(PHILIP *and* CAROLINE *turn to Harriet*)

PHILIP (*moving* RC) No! I thought I'd take a stroll in the moonlight before I turn in.

HARRIET. It's late and you are going to see the Italian first thing in the morning. You should be as fresh and rested as possible for the interview. May I remind you that we didn't come here for moonlight strolls but to rescue a child?

(*The light dies out of* CAROLINE'S *face to be replaced by a dull, remorseful look*)

CAROLINE (*in her Sawston voice*) I think we should all be turning in. Good night, Mr Herriton. (*She moves to the stairs*)

PHILIP. Good night. All right, Harriet, you have won. There's no need to go on standing there, glowering down like an Old Testament prophet.

(HARRIET *turns and exits at the top of the stairs*)

Blast her! (*He goes up* RC, *hangs his hat on the clothes hooks* L *of the door up* RC, *then moves to* R *of the table* C)

CAROLINE (*starting up the stairs*) No, she's quite right. (*She stops and turns. Wistfully*) But thank you, all the same. I should have enjoyed it.

CAROLINE *exits up the stairs.*

PHILIP *looks after Caroline for a moment then goes above the desk, turns out the gas bracket, crosses to* C, *turns out the gas bracket up* C, *moves* L, *glances once more out of the window at the moonlit tower then exits up the stairs as—*

the LIGHTS *dim to* BLACK-OUT

During the Scene Change a church bell is heard striking ten.

SCENE 3

SCENE—*Gino Carella's house, Monteriano. The following morning.*

It is one of those places that scrambles up a steep hill, producing storeys at all sorts of different levels. The main ground floor rooms are at the back, off a loggia R. *The loggia has a low stone parapet from which the land*

To face page 26—Where Angels Fear to Tread Photograph by Angus McBean *drops away precipitately; leagues of vineyards, olive orchards, hills and a cloudless sky, for a view. Adjoining it,* L, *is a room of which it seems simply an extension, since all the real living of the household is done in one or the other. The room and loggia are separated by a wall with an arch* C. *Up* L *of the loggia is a flight of steps, with a wooden door at the top, leading to the salone and kitchen. In the room* L, *there is a curtained arch up* R, *leading to other parts of the house. The entrance from the road is through an arch up* R *of the loggia. The loggia is furnished with a table* R *and a couple of dusty chairs above and below the table. The room* L *has a built-in cupboard and shelves* L; *a couch* LC; *a circular table* C *and two chairs, one up* R *and one down* R. *The room is in shocking disorder. Various articles of Gino's clothing are strewn about on chairs and floor; a pile of newspapers lie on the chair up* C, *an ashtray overflowing with cigar butts is on the table. It is a mess, but the mess that comes from living, not from apathy. Up* L, *on the wall of the room is a picture of Lillia, in a black frame, which is draped with black crêpe. The cupboard and shelves* L *are filled to overflowing with clothing and various odds and ends.*

When the LIGHTS *come up, the stage is empty. After a moment,* CAROLINE *enters up* R *in the loggia. She has added a wide-brimmed, summer hat to her costume of the preceding Scene. She looks like someone in a dentist's waiting-room, braced for the ordeal but uncertain of surviving it. She pauses on the loggia to look at the view and at the dirty crockery on the table. She moves to the foot of the steps, looks up them, then goes through the arch* C *into the room. She sees Lillia's picture on the wall up* L, *sighs, looks at the mess, including the trousers on the chair down* C, *turns, goes through the arch on to the loggia and stands* L *of the table, looking at the view off* R. GINO CARELLA *enters the living-room down stairs and through the arch. He is wearing his hat, smoking a cigar and whistling melodiously, a feat almost impossible for anyone but an Italian to accomplish. His profile is delicately modelled yet strong. Full face, he is less distinguished but quite as handsome. He is incapable of making a movement that is not full of vitality and grace. He is carrying a copper can of water. He puts the can on the chair up* R, *moves down* C, *takes off his hat, tosses it carelessly on to the chair down* R, *then moves to* R *of the couch, leans over it and addresses himself to a baby, who lies sleeping, swaddled in a light shawl, in a basket on the floor* L *of the couch.*

GINO. Stai bene?

(CAROLINE, *hearing Gino's voice, turns and crosses to the arch* C. *The baby is hidden from her by the couch, and she can only see Gino*)

CAROLINE (*in a low, timid voice*) Signor Carella . . .

(GINO, *with his back to Caroline, does not hear or see her*)

GINO (*to the baby*) A che profumo! Alza ti e prendi una tirata. (*He takes a packet of soap from his jacket pocket, removes his jacket, puts it on the chair down* R, *and takes the wrapping from the soap*) Come sei pigro.

(GINO *continues to address the baby, but to* CAROLINE *it appears that he is addressing "the little-man-who-wasn't-there". She moves in alarm to* RC *of the loggia*)

Dove andata Perfetta? Hai visto lei? Tu lo sai ma non voi dirmilo. Essatamente come te! (*He moves to* R *of the couch*) Che tipo!

(CAROLINE *gives a little cry of fright. She is pale, trembling and staring in horror at Gino*)

(*He whirls round and sees Caroline*) Signorina Abbott! (*He drops the soap on the table* C, *hastens out to Caroline and takes her hands*) But you tremble. What has happened? Something has frightened you?
CAROLINE. I—I am not feeling very well.

(GINO *pulls the chair below the table* R, *forward a little*)
I came here on business, but . . .
GINO. Business with me?
CAROLINE. Yes, but it can wait for some other time. (*She begins a hasty retreat towards the exit up* R) When you haven't a guest.
GINO (*with a step to stop her*) A guest? I do not understand. I have no guest but you.

(CAROLINE *casts a compulsive look into the empty room*)
(*He suddenly understands*) Ah! You hear me talking, you see no-one, you think . . . (*He taps his head expressively and bursts into laughter, which he checks swiftly. With solicitude and remorse*) Forgive me for laughing. I am desolated to frighten you. (*He takes Caroline's arm and leads her into the room*) Come! I will show you the person to whom I talked. (*He moves to* L *of the couch*)

(CAROLINE *moves* C *of the room*)
(*He lifts the basket and puts it on the downstage end of the couch, the head towards the audience*) There! My son.
CAROLINE. Oh! (*She stares at the baby, or rather what is visible of him, the back of his head, a dimpled left arm and two tiny bare feet*)
GINO (*with pride; softly*) My son, Vittorio.

(CAROLINE *tries to recover her poise by adopting the manner she uses when doing social work in Sawston*)

CAROLINE. What a fine child, Signor Carella. It's unusual to see such a head of hair at four months. And how nice of you to talk to him. Though I see the ungrateful little fellow is asleep.
GINO. I will wake him later. First we will talk. (*He crosses to* RC *of the room. In the tone of a hostess apologizing for a stray thread on the carpet*) It is a little untidy, this room, I am afraid. (*He moves to* R *of Caroline*) Let us go to the salone. It is always neat for I never use it except on the most important occasions. And it is always cool there for the windows are never opened. (*He goes out on to the loggia, up the steps and opens the door*)

(CAROLINE *goes through the arch on to the loggia, her dismay at this all-too-vivid picture just barely concealed*)

CAROLINE. Oh, but I think I prefer the sunshine.

GINO (*coming down the steps*) Ma certamente! (*He crosses to the chair below the table* R *and dusts it with his sleeve*) Wherever it pleases you. I am so glad you have come. (*He ushers Caroline to the chair*)

(CAROLINE *sits on the chair down* R)

(*He stands* R *of Caroline*) I regret that I could not speak longer with you yesterday, but I was on my way to take the omnibus to Poggibonsi. Had I missed it there was no other until today. (*He moves down* R) And I had urgent business in Poggibonsi. (*He seats himself on the parapet, one foot in the loggia, the other on the wall*)

CAROLINE (*perfunctorily*) I see.

GINO. Can you guess what it was, this urgent business?

CAROLINE. I'm afraid not.

GINO. But try.

CAROLINE (*with gentle sarcasm*) Perhaps you went to find something to do.

(GINO *looks blank*)

A job—Il lavoro.

GINO. No, no. (*With a gesture indicating the hopelessness of such a quest*) E manca questo. It is impossible to find suitable work. Make another guess, please.

CAROLINE. I cannot guess, Signor Carella. I am here, as I told you, on business.

GINO. But we are old friends. Your approval is grateful to me. You gave it to me once before. I hope for you to give it now.

CAROLINE. I have not come as a friend this time. I am not likely to approve of anything you do.

GINO (*laughing as if he found this a piquant jest*) Oh, signorina. Surely you approve of marriage?

CAROLINE. Do you mean that you intend to marry again?

GINO (*nodding*) Si! Everything has been agreed upon but the date. (*He smiles at Caroline, awaiting her congratulations*)

CAROLINE (*rising and standing above her chair; all the indignation of her sex and her nationality ringing in her voice*) You can't do it! I forbid you!

GINO (*petulantly*) But why?

CAROLINE. You have already destroyed Lillia. I won't allow you to destroy another woman.

GINO (*rising and moving to* R *of Caroline; indignantly*) I destroy my poor wife! I guarded her from all harm that could come to her. Soon after we were married I found that she took walks quite alone. This I put a stop *instamente*. Never again did I permit her to go out, without Perfetta, our servant, to accompany her.

CAROLINE. Did you also make her wear a veil over her face?

GINO. A veil? Ah—you joke with me.

CAROLINE. No, I am not joking. Did it ever occur to you to go walking with her yourself?

GINO. She wished it. But to walk without object . . . (*He spreads his hands hopelessly at the sheer unreasonableness of the request*) There were many things she did not understand. She wished me to bring my friends to dine with us, to play at cards. They would have thought me mad had I done so.

CAROLINE. Why?

GINO. My friends, signorina, are *men*.

CAROLINE. And have they no wives and sisters? Women that might have become Lillia's friends and company for her in some of those long hours you left her all by herself?

GINO. The wives and sisters of my friends I scarcely know. (*He sits on the down* L *corner of the table*) When one receives guests in one's own house, they are relatives. And my relatives—I love them but many of them are in trade, even my father is little more. (*He rises and moves down* R) My poor wife was accustomed to gentlefolk and nobility; it was not suitable for her to receive my family often, and this I explained to them.

CAROLINE. Without consulting Lillia's own wishes, I suppose. Just as you came and went as you pleased. Just as you used her money as you pleased, just as you . . .

(GINO's *face changes startlingly, round expressionless eyes in a cold mask, and his voice, though he does not raise it, has a quality that is frightening. He moves to* R *of Caroline and prods her shoulder*)

GINO. I was her husband, signorina. You forget that. So did she —at first. But she learnt to remember. (*As suddenly as it has appeared, this glimpse of brutality in him vanishes. He moves down* R *and sits on the wall. Plaintively*) Alora, you do not approve of my new marriage. But why?

CAROLINE (*moving to* L *of Gino*) I suppose the woman has money?

GINO (*nodding sulkily*) Si. Un' po. (*With thumb and forefinger he measures the smallness of his intended's fortune*)

CAROLINE. And I suppose you will say that you love her?

GINO. I will not say it. It is not true.

CAROLINE (*as, though reasoning with a child*) How can you expect a marriage to succeed where there is no love?

GINO. But there is. She loves me.

CAROLINE. Indeed!

GINO. Yes, yes. (*He lays his hand on his heart*) Passionately.

CAROLINE. Then God help her.

(GINO *jumps up, stamps his foot, moves to the table and stubs out his cigar in the ashtray*)

GINO. You are most unfair, signorina. All I say displeases you. You complain that there is no love in this marriage. I show you that there is and you are yet more angry. Che vuole? Do you think she

will not be content? (*He crosses above Caroline, goes through the arch into the room and stands up* L *of the table*) Glad she is to get me and she will do her duty well.
CAROLINE (*with a bitter cry*) Her duty! (*She crosses and goes through the arch into the room*)
GINO. But, yes. She knows why I marry her.
CAROLINE (*moving up* R *of the table*) To succeed where Lillia failed. To be your housekeeper, your slave.
GINO. To look after the baby, certainly.
CAROLINE. The baby?
GINO. Of course. I am having her for my son. Do you not understand?
CAROLINE (*after a pause; carefully*) I see. It won't be necessary, Signor Carella. (*She goes on to the loggia*)

(GINO *goes on to the loggia*)

If you find the baby too much trouble . . .
GINO. Please! Do not be unfair again. (*He leans against the downstage side of the arch* C) There is Perfetta, but she is old and careless. I dare not let her wash him. I feed him and sleep with him and comfort him when he is unhappy in the night. No-one may sing to him but I. These things I like to do. (*With a note of pathos*) But some are things not suitable for a young man.
CAROLINE. Not at all suitable. But marriage is a very serious step. If you would allow him to be cared for by—by relatives whom you can trust . . .
GINO. No, no! (*Putting the chair into the* L *side of the table*) My father and mother would live here gladly, but I will not have them. For they would separate us, my son and I.
CAROLINE. How?
GINO (*simply*) They would separate our thoughts.

(CAROLINE *looks at Gino in surprise and confusion, as the suspicion dawns on her that he really loves his son. There is a short silence*)

This woman from Poggibonsi will not do that. She will do only what I require. She is not beautiful—that I cannot pretend to you. But she is clean; she has fondness for children, her hands are gentle. (*His mood changes with the speed of lightning*) But you have not seen Vittorio yet. Come. (*He goes into the room and crosses to* R *of the couch*)
CAROLINE (*hanging back*) I have seen him, Signor Carella.
GINO. The top of his head. That is nothing. (*He lightly prods the basket with the toe of his shoe*) Wake up! We have a guest. (*He crosses below the sofa to* L *of it*)
CAROLINE. Oh, take care. (*She comes into the room*) You may hurt him. (*She puts her bag and gloves on the table and crosses to* R *of the couch*)
GINO (*proudly*) Not he. E duro. Yes, though he is small, he is strong. (*He gazes down at the baby*) Some day he will be larger than I am—higher. In only seventeen years, perhaps. Is it possible? (*He takes the baby from the basket*) It is time you were washed, lazy, dirty

one. (*He crosses and thrusts the baby in Caroline's arms*) Please hold him a minute. (*He moves the table and puts it down* L *of the arch* C, *then picks up the soap*)
CAROLINE (*startled*) You are going to wash him, now?
GINO. Perfetta has heated water I have bought new soap at the farmacia. You will excuse me. I can wait no longer. (*He moves to the arch up* R, *draws back the curtain and pulls on an old-fashioned tin hip-bath which he puts up* R *of the couch. He then gets the can of water from the chair up* R, *pours the water into the bath, tests the temperature with his finger, and nods*) I feared it had grown cold, but it is just as he likes it. (*He puts the can on the floor down* R *of the bath and drops the soap into the water*) At first he had the little basin for his bath but he grew too large for it. So now I most kindly allow him to use my own. (*He rolls up his sleeves, moves to Caroline and takes the baby from her*) I will take him from you now, signorina. Vieni, Vittorio. Come te adoro—tesoro mio!

(CAROLINE *turns to leave, collects her bag and gloves and goes on to the loggia*)

But why do you go? I will wash him while we talk.

(CAROLINE *stands irresolute*)

(*He turns his back to the audience, removes the shawl from the baby and puts it on the couch*) Now you will see how brown he is. Brown all over. Ah, che bellezza. And he is mine—mine for ever. (*He lifts the baby to his lips and kisses it with a passion that is far removed from nursery prettiness. At this instant he is majestic, he is Man saluting his own immortality*)

(CAROLINE *suddenly turns away, tears coming to her eyes*)

Even if he hates me, he is still mine. He cannot help it; he is made out of me, I am his father. (*He kneels* L *of the bath, with his back to the audience, and lowers the baby into it, keeping hold of the nape of the neck. The bath's high sides completely hide the baby from the audience*)
CAROLINE (*putting her bag and gloves on the loggia table*) Oughtn't you to soap him first? (*She removes her hat, puts it on the loggia table and comes into the room*)
GINO. Soap? Here is soap—very expensive soap, della farmacia.
CAROLINE (*humbly*) May I help you? (*She picks up the can, puts it on the chair up* R, *kneels* R *of the bath and puts her hand under the baby's head*)
GINO. Grazie, signorina. (*He rises and looks around for something to cover Caroline's dress*) But you will spoil your beautiful dress. Un momento.

(*The* BABY *squeals angrily*)

(*To the baby*) Silenzio! (*He picks up his jacket, moves to Caroline and ties it around her waist*) It is very kind of you to do this.

(CAROLINE *leans over the bath and washes the baby with the gentle motions of an expert baby-washer*)

(*He watches admiringly*) Perfetta washes him just as she washes clothes. (*He kneels on the couch*) And I require half the morning. (*To the baby*) Non sei fiero d'essere lavato della bella Signorina Inglese? (*He leans over and splashes the water in the bath*)

(*The* BABY *squeals*)

CAROLINE. Be careful of his eyes.
GINO. 'Scusi! Stai tranquillo, bambino mio. Zitto! Zitto!
CAROLINE. Could you get me a soft towel to dry him with?
GINO. Certainly, certainly. (*He rises and strides purposefully to the cupboard up* L)

(CAROLINE *continues her ministrations*)

(*He rummages helplessly through the cupboard, pulling out several unsuitable objects, before he holds up a silk shirt*) Will this shirt be of use to you? (*He crosses to Caroline*) It is very soft—of the purest silk. A present from my poor wife.
CAROLINE (*glancing over her shoulder at the shirt*) The water will spot it.
GINO (*with the shrug of a millionaire*) Non importa. (*He kneels* L *of Caroline and spreads the shirt on his knees*) Let me take him out. (*He lifts the baby from the bath, wraps it in the shirt and rises*)
CAROLINE (*rising*) Have you some baby powder? (*She dries her hands on the sleeve of the shirt*)
GINO (*striking his forehead*) Accidenti! Why did I not think when I am at the farmacia?
CAROLINE. It's not essential. (*She crosses to the couch, sits, picks up the shawl and spreads it on her lap*) It just makes them a little more comfortable.

(GINO *sings a lullaby as he dries the baby, then kneels above Caroline, puts the baby on the shawl, pulls away the shirt and throws it in the bath.* CAROLINE *wraps the baby in the shawl.* GINO *remains kneeling, gazing admiringly at Caroline and his son.*
PHILIP *enters up* R *on the loggia, moves* C *and takes in the three of them appreciatively. His arm still in a sling*)

PHILIP (*with spontaneous pleasure*) Madonna and child, with donor.
CAROLINE (*with a start*) Oh, Mr Herriton!
GINO (*jumping to his feet with quick grace*) Signor Filippo! (*He goes through the arch* C *to* L *of Philip, takes his hand and draws him into the room*) Enter, enter, I beg of you! When did you come to Monteriano?
PHILIP. Why—last night. (*He gives Caroline a surprised glance*)

(CAROLINE *busies herself with re-swaddling the baby in the shawl, keeping her eyes away from Philip's*)

GINO (*wringing Philip's hand*) Benvenuto! But you have hurt your arm?
PHILIP. Broken it. Not seriously, though. The sling is a nuisance, but that's the worst of it.
GINO (*taking Philip's hat*) Ah, the English! (*He moves to the chair*

down R, *puts his own hat on the floor, dusts the chair with his sleeve and puts Philip's hat on it*) Never do they complain when they suffer. Now if it is I who break an arm—che rumore! I weep, I shout, I say bad words—the baddest that I know. (*He moves to* R *of Philip*)

PHILIP. Much more satisfactory than our system. The stiff upper lip only benefits the sufferer's friends.

GINO (*moving the table to* C) We must have some wine. (*He takes the ashtray from the table, empties it into the bath and replaces it on the table*) To celebrate your arrival and to refresh the Signorina Abbott who has had much work washing my son. (*He crosses to Caroline*) I will take him from you now, signorina. (*He takes the baby from Caroline and puts it in the basket*) Soon he will be hungry and howl like a wolf. (*He picks up the basket with the baby in it and goes on to the loggia*) I will give him to Perfetta and fetch the wine—subito.

(GINO *exits up the steps with the baby*)

PHILIP. He's rather charming, isn't he? Not at all the way I remember him from the last time. Of course, he was in a position then where he was bound to show at a disadvantage—and I was angry. (*He looks at Gino's jacket still tied around Caroline's waist*)

(CAROLINE *hastily removes the jacket and lays it carefully over the end of the couch*)

I gather you haven't told him why we're here?
CAROLINE. No.
PHILIP (*moving down* R *of the table*) Well, you've put him in a good humour, anyway, and that will make my job easier. Washing his baby for him was a clever move.

(CAROLINE *looks up from smoothing out the sleeve of Gino's jacket*)

CAROLINE (*in sharp protest*) No!
PHILIP. What's the matter, Miss Abbott? Has anything happened to disturb you?
CAROLINE. I have found out something that I never knew before. I have found out that bad, worthless people are capable of love—of great love.

(PHILIP *stares searchingly at Caroline.*

PERFETTA *enters down the steps, carrying a tray with glasses and cakes. She comes into the room through the arch* C *and puts the tray on the table*)

PERFETTA. Buon giorno, signore e signorina.

(GINO *enters down the steps, carrying a glass decanter of white wine*)

GINO (*coming into the room*) You like Orvieto, I hope, Signor Filippo?
PHILIP. I do indeed.
GINO. The cakes are for you, signorina. Ladies enjoy to nibble something with their wine. (*To Perfetta*) Andate!

Scene 3   WHERE ANGELS FEAR TO TREAD   35

(PERFETTA *exits up the steps.* GINO *picks up a glass and pours wine*)

CAROLINE. I'm sorry. I must go now. (*She rises and moves towards the arch* C)

(GINO, *decanter and glass in hand, blocks her way*)

GINO. No, no, I will not permit you. You must taste the wine first. It is excellent.

(CAROLINE *shakes her head, mutely*)

Besides—you have not yet told me what is this "business" you come to discuss with me.

(CAROLINE *looks at Gino, tries to speak and bursts into tears. Still weeping, she runs past Gino on to the loggia, picks up her hat, bag and gloves and exits up* R. GINO *and* PHILIP *stare at one another, appalled, then* PHILIP *starts after Caroline and crosses to the exit up* R. GINO *puts the decanter and glass on the table and follows him, but Caroline has already disappeared round the corner of the house.* PHILIP *puts a restraining hand on Gino's arm*)

PHILIP. Better let her go.
GINO (*distressed*) Did I say something to offend her?
PHILIP. It wasn't that.
GINO. What, then?
PHILIP (*moving down* C *of the loggia*) I don't know. I can guess a little but I don't understand what I guess.
GINO (*moving to* R *of Philip; with a puzzled sigh*) She said she come on business. Then she forgot about it.
PHILIP. The business is really mine and my sister's—she's here with me. Miss Abbott is kindly helping us.
GINO. So? Alora, let us have our wine before we discuss it. (*He crosses above Philip to the arch*) Stay here, I bring it. (*He goes into the room and picks up the decanter and two glasses*)

(PHILIP *sits on the right end of the parapet, gazing at the view.* GINO *comes on to the loggia, pulls the chair from the table towards Philip, and puts the decanter and glasses on it*)

PHILIP. What a view to have for one's own.
GINO (*pouring wine*) You like it? Then you must come often and enjoy it. (*He hands a glass of wine to Philip, fills his own glass and holds it up in a toast*) Cheers!
PHILIP (*raising his glass*) Salute! (*He drinks*)

(GINO *watches anxiously*)

You are right. The wine is excellent.

(GINO's *mood has changed again. Once more he is the gay and charming host*)

GINO (*relieved*) I am glad it pleases you. It is recommended to me by the padrone of the *Café Garibaldi*, a most knowledgeable man.

(*He leans against the downstage side of the arch*) If you permit, I will take you to the *Garibaldi* and introduce you to my friends. There is always good company there. It is like English club.

PHILIP (*stretching luxuriously in the sunshine*) I'm sure it's much livelier, and more fun.

GINO. Friday night there will be a performance of *Lucia di Lammermoor* at the teatro. A company from Napoli, said to be very fine. Do you care for opera?

PHILIP. Very much—especially in Italy.

GINO. Then you and your sister and the Signorina Abbott must be my guests. I will take a box. Our teatro is not *La Scala*, but it is very pretty. Everything is red—the seats, the carpets, the walls, and there is a new curtain which is purple. (*He moves and picks up the decanter*) Also a great new chandelier, very modern, of all colours, like a window in a church. Magnifico! (*He refills Philip's glass*)

PHILIP. There's nothing I'd like better than to accept your invitation. *Grazie! Basta! Basta!*

(GINO *puts the decanter on the table, turns the chair and straddles it*)

If we are still here.

GINO (*facing Philip*) But Friday comes in only two more days. I know there is much else in Italy to see more important, but surely you can spend three days in Monteriano.

PHILIP. I could happily spend three months. (*He rouses himself with a sigh from the spell of the sun, the wine, and Gino's agreeable presence*) Unfortunately, we aren't here for pleasure, but only for the matter I came to discuss with you.

GINO. Ah, so. The business. Is it important business?

PHILIP. Yes—very.

GINO. Has it to do with money?

PHILIP. Yes.

GINO. Bene. Shall we proceed with it? (*He rises and goes into the room*)

PHILIP. I suppose we must.

(GINO *finishes his drink, puts the glass on the tray, collects his jacket from the couch and puts it on.* PHILIP *rises, finishes his drink, puts the glass on the loggia table and comes into the room*)

GINO. Vuole fumare?

PHILIP. *Grazie.*

(GINO *hands a cigar to Philip, from a tin on the tray, strikes a match on the table and lights it, then takes and lights a cigar for himself*)

GINO. Va bene. Let us go up to the salone. Is the proper place for the discussion of important business.

(GINO *crosses above Philip, goes up the steps and holds the door open for him as—*

the CURTAIN *falls*

ACT II

Scene 1

Scene—*The salone of the hotel. Noon, two days later.*

When the Curtain *rises, the shutters are open and the salone is brightly sunlit.* Signora Aletti *is behind the desk, writing in her ledger and occasionally consulting the calendar on the wall behind her.* Caroline *enters down* L *and crosses to* L *of the desk. She wears her hat and carries her handbag and a parasol.*

Signora Aletti. Buon giorno, Signorina Abbott.
Caroline. *Buon giorno, Signora Aletti. Vorrei prenderlo uno treno per Firenze domani mattino.*

(Harriet *enters down the stairs. She carries her key, a hat and her handbag*)

Signora Aletti. Domani mattino. Ma deve partire cosi presto, signorina?

(Harriet *crosses to the desk*)

Caroline. *Si. Quale e il migliore?* (*She turns*) Good morning, Harriet. (*She removes her hat and hangs it with her parasol and handbag on a peg* L *of the door up* RC)

(Harriet *hands her room key to Signora Aletti*)

Signora Aletti. Good morning, Mees 'Erriton. You sleep well? (*She hangs the key on the keyboard, then takes a time-table from the shelf under the desk, puts it on the left end of the desk and consults it*)
Harriet. Sleep? With all that racket going on outside? (*She crosses, slumps into the chair* L *of the table* C, *puts down her bag and hat and presses both hands to her forehead*)
Signora Aletti (*to Caroline*) Scusi?
Caroline. *La Signorina parla della festa.*
Signora Aletti (*beaming at Harriet*) Ah, la festa della Santa Deodata. It is our greatest religious celebration here. I am glad you enjoy it. (*She turns to Caroline*) C'e un solo treno al mattino e parte a le nove e mezza.
Caroline. *Tante grazie.*
Signora Aletti. Prego, signorina.
Caroline (*moving behind the chair* R *of the table*) Have you a headache, Harriet?
Harriet. A very bad one, dear. (*She shudders*) The children blowing bladder-whistles all night. And those dreadful street bands. Religious celebration! They're about as religious as the Hottentots.

(SIGNORA ALETTI *exits up* RC, *leaving the time-table on the desk*)

(*She takes her hands from her forehead*) What was all that about a train?
CAROLINE (*moving to the chair down* R) I'm leaving tomorrow morning. (*She sits*)
HARRIET. Leaving? Caroline! You mustn't! You can't desert us with nothing accomplished.
CAROLINE (*uncomfortably*) There's nothing more I can do to help you, Harriet.
HARRIET. That's not so. We never needed you more. Philip is completely useless. We've been here almost three days now and he's no closer to getting the baby than he was when we arrived. All his interviews with Carella have come to nothing. Mother was afraid of that—Philip is so absurd about Italy that any Italian can make a fool of him.
CAROLINE. I think you exaggerate Mr Herriton's helplessness.
HARRIET. No, I don't. Besides, he doesn't really care a straw if we get the baby. (*She fixes Caroline with a searching gaze*) You must see that yourself. Don't you?

(CAROLINE'S *silence is a reluctant affirmative*)

Of course you do. Well, there's nothing for it now but for us to take over.
CAROLINE. Us?
HARRIET. You and I. That man respects you, Philip says. And he'll soon see that I'm not the sort who can be put off with excuses.
CAROLINE. Harriet—haven't you wondered why Signor Carella should put us off with excuses if he doesn't care about his child and is only interested in getting money for it?
HARRIET. I suppose he enjoys bargaining—all Latins do.
CAROLINE. Now, really, Harriet . . .
HARRIET (*interrupting*) We'll go and see him this afternoon. Just the two of us. (*She rises and moves* C, *her voice a battle-cry, her face stern and confident*) We'll tell him we've had enough of shilly-shallying. We'll demand the child of the woman he murdered. Together we're bound to succeed. (*In a less exalted tone*) Just after lunch would be best. He's sure to be home then, having his siesta.
CAROLINE. I can't do it, Harriet. I can't help you in any way. You see, I've changed sides.

(HARRIET *stares at Caroline, not yet understanding*)

I think your mission—our mission, it was, at first—will fail. And I think it deserves to fail because it is a bad mission.
HARRIET (*glacially*) Would you make yourself a little clearer? Am I to take it that you now want Lillia's baby to remain with that scoundrel?
CAROLINE. With its father, who loves it.
HARRIET (*with a sound of fury and disgust*) Rubbish!
CAROLINE (*quietly, but with passionate conviction*) Gino has a great

many faults but he does love his son deeply. To try and part them is an unnatural act—therefore it's a wrong one. We have all been wrong, Harriet. (*She rises and takes a step towards Harriet*) Won't you try to understand?

(CAROLINE *is pleading with Harriet now, but nothing could be vainer.* HARRIET *has listened to her with growing outrage and not the slightest comprehension of her meaning*)

HARRIET. I understand all right! I understand that we've trusted a traitor! A turncoat! A liar!

CAROLINE. You have every right to be angry with me, but I haven't lied to you.

HARRIET. You have. From the very start. Lies, lies, lies about wanting to help us, when all the time you were working against us. And now this story that you're sorry for *him*. You called him "Gino" just then—oh, you disgust me. You disgust me.

(PHILIP *enters hurriedly down* L)

PHILIP. Harriet, please! I heard you from across the piazza.

(CAROLINE *moves below the desk*)

HARRIET. I don't care if the whole town hears me. (*She points at Caroline*) Do you know what that woman has just admitted? *Boasted* of?

CAROLINE. No, Harriet, not boasted.

PHILIP (*crossing below Harriet to the clothes-hooks up* RC) Ladies, please, it's far too hot for quarrelling. (*He hangs up his hat*) I suggest that each of you retire to her room with a book, until luncheon.

HARRIET. I'll never sit down at the same table with her again. She's betrayed us. She got hold of mother's plans and came to Monteriano deliberately to thwart them.

PHILIP (*moving down* RC) Nonsense!

HARRIET. Ask her! Ask her! We're to go away without the baby, because she won't let us take it from *him*—from its dear, sweet father.

(PHILIP *turns to Caroline*)

CAROLINE (*to Philip*) It's true that I've changed right round in my ideas. But I haven't done anything to prevent your getting the child, nor shall I. I'm going away tomorrow.

HARRIET (*witheringly, but the peak of her fury has passed*) Running away. (*She picks up her handbag from the table and rummages in it*) All treacherous people are cowards.

PHILIP (*moving to* R *of Harriet; sharply*) That's enough, Harriet!

HARRIET (*turning on Philip; close to tears*) And you're almost as bad. You spend hours and hours with him and his awful friends at that café. Oh, I've seen you, laughing and chattering and waving your arms the way they do. You're going to the opera with him—and you even told him that *I* might come. As though I'd accept his invitation to anything.

PHILIP. All right, all right, I'll tell him you refuse to go. I have another interview with him at noon. Do you want to unfit me for it with your hysterics? For goodness' sake, try and calm yourself. You'll bring on one of your headaches if you don't.

HARRIET (*pressing her hat to her forehead; in a wail*) I *have* a headache. And I've run out of phenacetin.

PHILIP. You'd better go and buy some at the farmacia and then lie down until luncheon.

(HARRIET *picks up her hat*)

CAROLINE (*crossing to* R *of the table*) I've got some, Harriet.

HARRIET. No, thank you, Miss Abbott. (*She puts on her hat, picks up her handbag and crosses to* L)

PHILIP (*crossing to* R *of Harriet*) I'd go for you if I hadn't got this meeting with Gino.

HARRIET (*with dull reproach*) You call him by his Christian name, too.

PHILIP. He's not the sort of chap one can stay formal with. Cheer up, Harriet! He hasn't said "yes", yet, but he hasn't said "no", either. Perhaps I'll be able to bring him round today.

HARRIET (*tonelessly*) Do your best.

(HARRIET *exits down* L, *walking heavily, with shoulders slumped*)

PHILIP (*turning to Caroline*) I'm afraid she won't apologize to you herself, so let me do it for her.

CAROLINE. I deserved most of it. It's natural that both of you should resent me.

PHILIP. But *I* don't. Not in the least. (*He crosses to* L *of Caroline*) You began to change the morning you were at his house and saw him with the baby, didn't you?

(CAROLINE *nods*)

That's why you went away so suddenly—I didn't understand then, but I do now.

CAROLINE. Do you?

PHILIP. I think so. He's made you believe that he loves the child.

CAROLINE. Yes—he has.

PHILIP. Well, we shall see. But to Harriet you have simply deserted the crusade, which makes you almost as bad as the enemy. And you can't expect her to believe that the enemy has the feelings you attribute to him. How could she when she has never loved a human being herself—only God and Duty and the Right? Well, perhaps she loved mother once—or would have if it had been reciprocated; she is still very anxious for mother's approval.

CAROLINE. You understand her very well, too.

PHILIP. I think I understand all your viewpoints in this affair: yours, hers, Gino's—even my mother's.

CAROLINE. If you understand Signor Carella, then you know this interview today will come to nothing—like all the others.

Scene I   WHERE ANGELS FEAR TO TREAD   41

PHILIP. Why does he go on with them, I wonder, if he's already made up his mind?

CAROLINE. He thinks it's politer, he likes your company—perhaps it amuses him to keep us all hanging about, waiting on his decision. (*She turns away down* R) But you will never persuade him to part with his son.

PHILIP. I could have persuaded him to part with Lillia, if he hadn't already married her. The look in his eyes when I mentioned the cash I was prepared to give was unmistakable—pure greed and regret that it was too late.

CAROLINE. He didn't love Lillia. The child is part of himself.

PHILIP. Well, you may be right. In fact, I'm almost sure you are.

CAROLINE (*moving to behind the chair* R *of the table*) So what are you going to do?

PHILIP. Do? Why, see him today and if this interview fails, see him again tomorrow. (*He sits* L *of the table*) I can see the humour of the situation. Gino sitting up on his mountain-top with his cub. We come and ask for it. He welcomes us. We ask for it again. He is equally pleasant. I'm agreeable to spend the whole week bargaining with him. If we fail in the end, we shall at least fail honourably.

CAROLINE (*with sudden, splendid scorn*) That's not doing anything. You would be doing something if you kidnapped the baby or if you took Harriet straight away from here. But to "fail honourably"—to come out of the thing as well as you can—is that all you are after?

PHILIP (*disconcerted*) Why—yes, frankly, that's exactly what I'm after. I've never pretended to care about getting the baby as Harriet does and you do—I mean as you *did*. Really, Miss Abbott, it's rather difficult to follow you through all your turns of feeling.

CAROLINE. I don't expect you to. But I do expect you to settle what's right and follow that.

PHILIP. Right for whom? It depends, you know.

CAROLINE (*with passion*) The child is the only person who matters. (*She turns away down* R) None of us have thought of him as a person, that's the trouble. To Harriet, he's a brand to be snatched from the burning; to Mrs Herriton, he's a necessary prop to sustain her reputation for kindness and generosity; to me—(*she hesitates; painfully*) I realize now that I only wanted him brought to England to ease my bad conscience about Lillia—to make me able to forget my guilt. I was just as uncaring and dishonest as your mother.

PHILIP. No, you weren't. You are incapable of conscious dishonesty.

CAROLINE. The unconscious kind does just as much harm. No, until the morning when I went to see Gino, I thought of the child as abstractedly as the rest of you. But he is a human being; he can grow up happy or unhappy. (*She moves to* R *of the table and faces Philip across it*) Look! (*She looks challengingly at him*) Do you want him to remain with his father, who loves him, and will bring him up badly or go to Sawston where nobody loves him and he will be brought up well? There is the question, put dispassionately enough even for you. Settle it. Decide which side you're on and fight for it. But *don't* talk about—(*she raps the table and turns away down* R) "failing honourably". That's just an excuse for not thinking or acting at all.

PHILIP. You are a wonderful person, Miss Abbott.

CAROLINE. Oh, you appreciate me. You appreciate us all. You recognize our good points and see through our pretensions to be good. But what's the use of fair-mindedness if you never decide anything for yourself? What's the use of insight if you never act on what you see? I'm slow-thinking and muddle-headed and not worth a quarter of you, but I try to do what seems right at the time; I don't sit on a chair, watching things happen as though I were at the theatre. (*She moves to* R *of the table*) Look, why don't you get angry with me?

PHILIP. I'm too interested in what you're saying.

CAROLINE. "Interested!" (*She sits* R *of the table*) You are dead—dead—dead.

(CAROLINE *has finally succeeded in hurting* PHILIP *but he only quotes wryly*)

PHILIP. "The grave's a fine and private place."

(CAROLINE'S *mood changes abruptly. She impulsively takes Philip's uninjured hand in hers*)

CAROLINE. I can't bear to see you wasted, Mr Herriton. You are such a fine person that I can't bear it. She has not been good for you, your mother.

PHILIP (*touched; almost tenderly*) Miss Abbott, don't worry over me. Some people are born not to do things, and I am one of them. I never did anything at school or at the university or at the *beaux-arts*. I call myself an architect but I am really doing nothing now. I came out here before intending to stop Lillia's marriage and it was too late. I've come out again, intending to get the baby and unless I'm very much mistaken I shall return "an honourable failure". I seem fated to pass through the world without colliding with it or moving it. I don't die—I don't fall in love. And if other people die or fall in love they always do it when I'm just not there.

CAROLINE. I wish something would happen to you, my dear friend.

PHILIP. I never expect it to any more, so I'm never disappointed. You would be surprised to know what my great moments are: the festa last night; laughing with Gino and his friends; talking to you now. You are quite right: life to me is just a spectacle, which—thank God and thank Italy and thank you—is more beautiful and heartening today than it has ever been.

CAROLINE (*repeating gravely*) I wish something would happen to you.

PHILIP. But why? (*He smiles at her*) Prove to me why I don't do as I am.

Scene 1   WHERE ANGELS FEAR TO TREAD

CAROLINE (*rising*) I can't prove it. And I can't prove why you shouldn't have any more interviews with Signor Carella but should tell Harriet that it's useless and bundle her into a carriage and drive her straight away. But I know that's what you ought to do. (*She moves up* RC *and collects her hat, parasol and handbag*)

PHILIP. Perhaps. But it isn't a very big "ought". Nothing hangs on it.

CAROLINE (*moving to* R *of the table*) I suppose I *am* extreme—I've been trying to run you as your mother does. Only every little trifle seems important today, and there's never any knowing which of our actions, which of our apathies, won't have something hanging on it, for ever. (*She moves behind the desk, collects the room key, then glances up at the clock*) Are you meeting Signor Carella at the *Garibaldi?*

PHILIP. No, he's coming here.

CAROLINE. Oh. Then he'll be here any second. (*She crosses hurriedly to the foot of the stairs*)

PHILIP. Aren't you going to wait and speak to him?

CAROLINE (*curtly*) Why should I? I have no more business with him.

PHILIP (*a little surprised at her tone*) Even so, he'd be pleased. He admires you very much.

CAROLINE. I have no wish ever to see him or speak to him again.

PHILIP (*rising and moving to* R *of the stairs; dismayed*) But the opera. If you don't care whether you disappoint him, think of me.

(CAROLINE *turns, undecided*)

I've been looking forward to tonight, like a child and half the fun will be spoiled if you don't come along.

CAROLINE. So have I been looking forward to it. (*As though debating with herself*) After all, it's my last night here . . . (*She hesitates then capitulates*) Very well, I'll come. (*She goes up the stairs*)

PHILIP (*calling up to her*) Splendid! I promise you won't regret it.

(CAROLINE *exits up the stairs.* PHILIP, *standing* C, *with his back to the exit down* L, *takes cigarettes and matches from his pocket, fits a cigarette into his holder, puts his case back in his pocket, then tries awkwardly to remove a match from the box*)

Oh, damn the things!

(GINO *enters noiselessly down* L, *unobserved by* PHILIP. *He is smoking a cigar. He takes in Philip's difficulties at a glance, takes a match from his pocket, strikes it on the stool* L, *then crosses to* L *of Philip*)

GINO. Permeso, Fra Filippo.

(PHILIP *jumps violently and turns*)

PHILIP. Good Lord, Gino, you gave me a start. Have you got Redskins in your ancestry?

GINO (*taking the cigarette and holder from Philip*) Redskins? American savages? (*He lights the cigarette*) I have an uncle in the city of Chicago but he is no savage—he is padrone of a fine ristorante.

D

(PHILIP *smiles, turns away and pockets his matches*)

Ah, it is a joke. Explain, Filippo. I love English jokes but I am not quick to understand them.

PHILIP. This one isn't worth the trouble.

(GINO *hands Philip the lighted cigarette*)

Thank you very much. It would have taken me ten minutes to do that myself.

GINO. Poveretto! But it will not be long before the bad arm mends. (*He indicates his cigar*) I do not offer you one of these, for I know that you detest them.

(PHILIP *looks guilty*)

(*He laughs at Philip's guilty expression*) How bravely, how politely you have smoked them, when all the time ... (*He makes a face of disgust, holds his nose, then puts his arm around Philip's shoulder*) It was wrong of me to let you suffer so long, but I could not help myself. I am a wicked man.

PHILIP. You are. A brute.

GINO. Let us go to the *Garibaldi* and I will buy you a vermouth to show that I repent of my wickedness. (*He moves down* L)

PHILIP (*firmly*) No, Gino. The *Garibaldi* is too distracting. Today, we're going to stick to the point.

GINO (*turning*) Come?

PHILIP (*assuming a blunt, no-nonsense manner*) It's been very pleasant, this fencing match, but it really won't do, you know. We must settle the matter, one way or the other.

(GINO *has been looking at Philip with bafflement until the end of the above speech. Now a gleam of amused comprehension comes into his eyes*)

GINO. Ah, yes. We are not here for pleasure but to do business.

PHILIP (*after a suspicious glance; brusquely*) Sit down. (*He indicates the chair* L *of the table, then sits* R *of the table*)

(GINO *removes his hat and crosses to* L *of the table*)

As the Americans say, you must fish, cut bait or get out of the boat.

(GINO *looks at Philip*)

That means make a decision and act on it. Now. At once.

(GINO *kisses his finger, touches the picture of Santa Deodata, then sits* L *of the table*)

GINO. They are most business-like, the Americans. That is why women admire them. (*With a sly grin*) Women also like to—how did you say—(*he imitates Philip's gruff, curt tones*) "Settle the matter".

(PHILIP *represses a smile with some difficulty*)

Is it the orders of your sister you follow, Filippo? Or those of the Signorina Abbott?

PHILIP (*with a last attempt at severity*) Don't dodge the issue, please. I . . .

GINO (*putting his hat on the table*) Women do not understand the pleasures of discussion. If they had their way every question would be answered *instamente* by "yes" or "no". And now you are in disgrace with them because you behave like a civilized man. Oh, poor Filippo! (*He begins to laugh, gasping, and wiping the tears from his eyes. He rises, slaps Philip on the shoulder, then resumes his seat*)

(PHILIP *watches Gino stiffly for a second, then his lips twitch and he grins sheepishly*)

PHILIP. Very well—I admit it. The ladies *are* managing this affair.

GINO (*tilting his chair back*) Ah, the ladies, the ladies. And the time we waste over them is much. (*He shakes his head indulgently and settles forward comfortably in his chair*) Naturalmente, you have always known, Filippo, that I could not be parted from my son. You are too sensible to believe the fantasia that I would exchange him for money. And me, I have always known that you are here only to please your mother, your sister, the Signorina Abbott.

PHILIP. That's largely true.

GINO. And happy I am that you wished to please them, for otherwise you would not have come to Monteriano and become my friend. Because I owe our friendship to the ladies, I am sorry they must be disappointed.

PHILIP. Miss Abbott won't be disappointed. She has come to realize that you could not do without your son—nor he without you.

GINO (*pleased*) She is molto simpatica, the Signorina Abbott.

PHILIP. As for the other two ladies—well, I have done my best. I shall face my mother with a good conscience. Will you bear me witness that I have done my best?

GINO (*placing a sympathetic hand on Philip's shoulder*) My poor fellow, I will. I will swear so.

(*They both laugh.*
HARRIET *enters down* L *on this comradely laughter.* PHILIP *sees her and hastily rises, like a schoolboy caught talking when he should be studying*)

PHILIP (*to Gino; sotto voce*) Mia sorella.

(GINO *springs to his feet*)

Harriet, you haven't met Signor Carella yet, have you? Gino—my sister, Miss Herriton.

GINO (*moving down* C; *with his customary grace of manner*) Miss Herriton, is a very great pleasure. (*He takes her hand and attempts to kiss it*)

(HARRIET *snatches her hand away, crosses to the desk, collects her key from the board, then goes below the desk.* PHILIP *and* GINO *turn to look at her*)

PHILIP (*nervously*) Did you get the stuff for your headache?

(HARRIET *nods*)

(*He explains to Gino*) My sister is suffering from a migraine.

GINO. Ah, there is nothing so bad as the migraine. I hope that it leaves you quickly.

(HARRIET *makes no reply*)

(*He glances at the clock and feigns dismay*) Miss Herriton, Filippo, excuse me, please. (*He collects his hat*) I am already in ritardo for an appointment. I must hurry. (*He moves down* L *and turns*) You will not forget that the opera commences at eight o'clock?

PHILIP. Indeed I won't.

GINO. I will call for you a little before. Good-bye until then.

(GINO *exits down* L. *There is a short silence*)

HARRIET (*looking at Philip*) Well?

PHILIP (*as kindly as he can*) I pressed him for a definite answer, Harriet, and he gave it to me. It was "no".

HARRIET (*without any expression at all*) I knew that. I knew it directly I saw you laughing together.

PHILIP (*gently*) It wouldn't have helped to quarrel with him.

HARRIET. You are sure he meant it?

PHILIP. Entirely sure. He couldn't have been more final.

(*There is a pause*)

HARRIET (*moving to* L *of the desk*) Then we should leave as soon as possible. (*She picks up the time-table from the desk and studies it*) There must be a train tonight—yes, there is. At midnight.

PHILIP. It's a very bad train, Harriet. We won't get to Florence until the small hours.

HARRIET (*replacing the time-table on the desk*) I can't help that. (*She moves down* R) It's unfair to mother to stop on, wasting her money, now that we've failed.

PHILIP. Our rooms are paid for tonight, in any case. There's a good train in the morning.

HARRIET. Caroline Abbott is taking that one. I really can't bring myself to speak to her, after what she's done, and it would be awkward travelling together all that way.

PHILIP. It certainly would be, if you're determined to snub her. (*He sighs*) All right, we'll leave tonight.

HARRIET. You won't have to miss the opera, if you pack this afternoon. There'll be plenty of time before the train leaves.

PHILIP (*crossing to* L *of Harriet; pleased and astonished at this thoughtfulness*) Why, thank you, Harriet. I do want awfully to see it.

HARRIET. I suppose Caroline will go with you?
PHILIP. Yes, she's promised to come. (*He puts his hand on Harriet's shoulder*) You're taking our failure very well, my dear. I know how it must disappoint you. (*Offstage up* R, *in the dining-room, a bell rings*)
HARRIET (*pulling away and crossing to the stairs*) I had better start packing. I shan't come down to luncheon. Will you ask the landlady to send up a cup of clear *consommé* and some biscuits?
PHILIP. Are you sure that's all you want?
HARRIET (*nodding*) Coming back from the chemist I felt so ill that I had to go into that church and sit down. At least it was cool there. (*She presses her hands to her forehead*)
PHILIP (*moving below the table*) But if you feel as bad as that, we certainly shouldn't try to travel tonight.
HARRIET. I shall be all right, by then. (*She takes her hands from her forehead. Resolutely*) I must be. (*She starts up the stairs, straightening her shoulders with an effort, gripping the rail and speaking as though she were exhorting herself*) My head is very bad but I can't give in to it. I mustn't.

HARRIET *exits up the stairs.* PHILIP *moves to the desk, stubs out his cigarette in the ashtray on it, then exits up* R *as—*

the LIGHTS *dim to* BLACK-OUT

SCENE 2

SCENE—*The same.* *11.15 p.m. the same night.*
 The Scene opens with the set completely dark and silent for several seconds. Then, from the blackness comes the distant sound of SIGNORA ALETTI, *singing an aria from* "*Lucia di Lammermoor*". *The voice grows closer, and the set lights up.*

When the LIGHTS *come up, the salone is empty. The gas bracket behind the desk is lit, as is the lamp on the stairs. The gas bracket* C *is dim. Moonlight streams through the open shutters.* SIGNORA ALETTI *enters down* L, *still singing. She is arrayed in such splendour as to be barely recognizable: cerise evening gown, with full decolletage; ear-rings like chandeliers; high-heeled satin slippers and a maribou boa. She carries a programme, an evening bag and a sequinned fan. It is obviously that she has been to the opera and is still happily beneath its spell, although her slippers are pinching her*)

SIGNORA ALETTI (*singing as she limps to the table* C) "Regnara nel silenzio, alta la notte e bruna . . ." (*She puts her bag, fan and programme on the table, removes one slipper, rubs her foot, and still singing, crosses to the chair down* R, *sits, puts the slipper on the floor below the chair, breaks off the song and gives a long sigh of satisfaction and relief*) Ah-hh!

(HARRIET *enters down the stairs. She wears her hat and travelling dress, and looks tense and curiously furtive. She carries a note in an envelope*)

HARRIET (*to the signora; in a low voice*) Has the carriage come for the *stazione*? (*She moves* C)
SIGNORA ALETTI (*rising*) Not yet, but I see the driver at the teatro and tell him come now. Ah, signorina, what a pity that you miss *Lucia*. Cera una meraviglia.
HARRIET (*cutting her short*) Listen carefully, please. When the driver comes tell him to take his carriage round to the back entrance.
SIGNORA ALETTI. Scusi?
HARRIET. La *porta—la porta indietro*. (*She gestures towards the door up* RC) Then he is to carry our *bagagli* down the back staircase and put it in the carriage, *porta indietro—scala indietro*. You understand?
SIGNORA ALETTI (*puzzled*) Si, signora. He is to put his carozza at the back and to descend the bagagli also by the back?
HARRIET. That's right. (*She glances nervously towards the exit down* L, *moves to the signora and thrusts the envelope into her hand*) Give this to Mr Herriton as soon as he comes in.

(HARRIET *turns and exits hurriedly up the stairs. The* SIGNORA *stares after her, then shrugs. After all, who has ever understood the ways of the English. She then limps up* C, *turns up the gas bracket and picks up the bag, fan and programme.*

CAROLINE *and* PHILIP *enter down* L. *They also carry programmes.* PHILIP *is talking with gay animation.* CAROLINE *is laughing and pleasure has made her radiant. The* SIGNORA *looks approvingly at them and moves down* R)

PHILIP (*as they enter*) . . . and the look of surprise and delight the *prima donna* gave—

(*The* SIGNORA *picks up her slipper, moves up* RC, *puts her fan, etc., on the stool and struggles back into the slipper.* CAROLINE *is* LC *and* PHILIP *down* L)

—when they wheeled on that extraordinary bamboo clothes-horse with the same shabby artificial flowers she gets at every performance.
CAROLINE (*laughing*) I should never have known, if you hadn't told me. But she got some real bouquets—from real admirers.
PHILIP. She did indeed! And she deserved them. (*He crosses below Caroline to* C. *To the Signora*) Signora! La Lucia aviva una voce molto bella.

(CAROLINE *moves to the table* C *and puts down her programme and bag*)

SIGNORA ALETTI (*moving down* RC) Ah, si! Bella come la primavera.
CAROLINE (*sitting* L *of the table*) Superba!
SIGNORA ALETTI. Che passione, che ardore quando cantava. (*She sings several bars from "The Mad Song", demonstrating the passion and fire she has admired, with suitable gestures and expressions*) "Edgardo! Edgardo! . . . Etc."
PHILIP. Bravissimo! You should sing in opera yourself, signora.
SIGNORA ALETTI (*with a deprecating laugh*) Fandonie, signore.

Ma lei e molto gentile. (*She turns to go, then suddenly remembers the envelope she has been waving about wildly in her rendition of "The Mad Song" is for Philip*) Ah, scusi tante. Ho dimenticato questo. Dalla sua sorella.
PHILIP (*puzzled*) Da mia sorella? Ma—dove?
SIGNORA ALETTI (*pointing up the stairs*) Lei e sopra.

(*The* CAB DRIVER *enters down* L, *carrying his whip. He, too, is singing an aria from "Lucia" in a resonant bass. He crosses to* LC)

(*She limps across to the Cab Driver*) A Peppi! Peppino!

(CAROLINE *takes the envelope from Philip, opens it and extracts the note*)

Lei deve condurre la sua carozza alla porta indietro.
CAB DRIVER. La porta indietro? Ma perche?
SIGNORA ALETTI La Signorina Inglese lo desidera. Venga!

(*The* CAB DRIVER *moves to the exit down* L. PHILIP *listens with perplexity*)

Le faro vedere dove; andiamo in sieme, attento le scalinette . . .

(*The* CAB DRIVER *exits down* L.
SIGNORA ALETTI *follows him off*. CAROLINE *hands the note to* PHILIP *who quickly reads it*)

PHILIP (*exasperated*) Really, this is going too far. (*To Caroline; with embarrassment*) She's afraid if she "encountered" you, she couldn't "control her feelings". So she's leaving the hotel by the back door in order to "avoid any unpleasantness", as she puts it.
CAROLINE. Oh. So that's why the driver was told to go round the back.
PHILIP. Apparently. Her note asks me to meet her there.
CAROLINE. I knew she stayed upstairs at luncheon and dinner to avoid me. Her feelings are understandable. This has been a terrible blow to her. And from what you tell me, she's taken it amazingly well.
PHILIP. So well that I've found it hard to believe she was herself. But this back door business reassures me. (*He crumples the note, moves to down* L *of the desk and throws the note angrily over the desk into the wastepaper basket*) Oh, well—(*he moves* C) I suppose I'd better go and join her. Good-bye.

(CAROLINE *smiles a little at Philip's annoyance, rises and holds out her hand*)

CAROLINE. Good-bye.

(PHILIP *takes her hand*)

And don't let anything spoil this wonderfully happy evening.
PHILIP. I don't think anything could. (*He gazes at Caroline for a*

second in silence, then releases her hand) Gino was at his absolute best, wasn't he?
CAROLINE. Yes, he was very nice. Oh, I enjoyed everything. The audience humming the arias with the singers and calling out congratulations to their relatives in the chorus—the gilt nymphs that held up that enormous clock on the proscenium—all the absurd things, as well as the beautiful ones.
PHILIP. In Italy the absurd has the confidence of beauty. Those plump young ladies with their clock would nod to the young men on the ceiling of the Sistine.

(HARRIET *enters down the stairs. She is breathing hard and her face shows every sign of panic*)

HARRIET (*as she descends*) Philip. Will you . . . ? (*She breaks off, looks at Caroline, hesitates, then fear overcoming enmity, she addresses Caroline jerkily*) Perhaps *you'd* know—you've had experience with them—your district work . . .
CAROLINE (*turning to Harriet; sharply*) What are you talking about?
HARRIET. If you'd come upstairs and have a look at the baby . . .
CAROLINE. The baby! (*She moves quickly to the stairs*)
HARRIET. Something seems wrong with it.

(CAROLINE *races up the stairs and exits at the top*)

I can't . . . (*She turns to follow Caroline*)

(PHILIP *moves quickly to Harriet, grabs her left wrist and pulls her down* L *of the table*)

PHILIP. What baby?
HARRIET (*stammering with fright*) His—at least, it's ours, now. I finally persuaded him—Carella—this afternoon—while you were packing . . .
PHILIP. Stop lying!
HARRIET. He wanted it to be a surprise for you. Caroline wasn't to know because she might have made a fuss. His—servant brought it tonight, while . . .
PHILIP (*shaking her arm violently*) What have you done to it?

(HARRIET's *face begins to twitch and she whimpers*)

HARRIET. You're hurting me. I didn't hurt it. I put it to rest in my own bed. I soothed it to sleep. Only somehow—it may have been when I came down here to give the landlady a note for you—it must have wriggled down under the covers then.

(PHILIP *releases Harriet's arm, lets out his breath sharply and crosses to the stairs.*
    CAROLINE *enters on the stairs.* PHILIP *halts and looks at her*)

I don't know how it managed—such a *small* baby.
CAROLINE (*answering Philip's unspoken question*) There is nothing anyone can do up there. (*She comes down the stairs*)

HARRIET (*with a scream of pure hysteria*) I stole it! I stole it! But I didn't hurt it. I carried it home gently in my arms. (*She demonstrates grotesquely, striding to* RC)

(PHILIP *and* CAROLINE *watch numbly*)

I went there while you were all at the opera. His servant was asleep in the kitchen. I stole past her and stole it—(*she gives a horrible laugh and flings herself into the chair* R *of the table*) stole past her and stole it——

(CAROLINE *crosses to* R *of Harriet*)

—(*she hugs herself and rocks back and forth, chuckling insanely*) stole past her and stole . . .

PHILIP *is frozen. The church bell strikes twelve as—*

the LIGHTS *dim to* BLACK-OUT

SCENE 3

SCENE—*Gino's house. Half an hour later.*

When the LIGHTS *come up, the scene is empty. The loggia is partly in moonlight, partly in shadow. An oil-lamp, turned down very low, is on the table in the room. A light wind sighs in the olive orchards below. After a few moments,* PHILIP *enters hurriedly up* R *in the loggia. He is hatless. He looks around, goes up the steps and opens the door.*

PHILIP (*calling softly*) Gino. Gino? Perfetta? (*He closes the door, comes down the steps, looks into the room, sees it is empty, moves* C, *shifts restlessly towards the exit up* R, *turns, moves slowly down* L *of the loggia and forces himself to resume his stiff, erect immobility*)

(GINO *enters up* R *in the loggia. His hat is at its usual dashing angle and he is swinging a short cane, which he uses only for formal occasions like the opera*)

GINO (*startled*) Chi e? (*He moves* C *and recognizes Philip*)

(PHILIP *turns*)

(*With surprise and pleasure*) Filippo! (*He moves to* R *of Philip*)
PHILIP. I went to the *Garibaldi* but you had just left.
GINO. Ah, yes, I stopped for a minute at the house of a friend. So you did not take the train. I am so happy. How desolate I was when I said good-bye to you at the teatro. Come in.
PHILIP (*catching Gino by the arm*) Not yet. I have something to tell you.
GINO (*gaily*) Certainly you shall tell me—(*he puts his cane against the chair below the table* R) we have the whole night before us. But I

must first see if Perfetta has heated the milk for my son He must be fed at a quarter past midnight, and . . .

PHILIP. The milk will not be needed now, Gino. (*He keeps his hold on Gino's arm*) The baby is dead. My sister came here, while we were at the opera and took him away. She did not mean to harm him. But he slipped down under the bedclothes and was smothered.

(GINO *has listened without any expression at all to this. He remains silent.* PHILIP *releases his arm.* GINO *goes into the room, stands above the table and turns the lamp up as full as it can go*)

(*He follows to* R *of Gino*) My sister has had a mental breakdown and Miss Abbott is guiltless.

(GINO *removes his hat and puts it on the table with his gloves*)

If I hadn't been indolent and trivial, I would have taken my sister away as soon as I knew our mission had failed—and I knew that, really, the first time I talked to you.

(GINO *crosses, kneels by the baby's basket and begins to feel the inside of it, as though he were blind.* PHILIP *watches him, controlling his agitation. Frowning a little,* GINO *rises and moves to the chair down* R)

(*He moves down* C) Gino! (*He crosses to* L *of Gino and puts his hand gently on his shoulder*)

(GINO *twitches away from Philip's touch, moves up* R *and makes terrible, blind, sweeping movements of his hands over the chair up* R, *over the wall, knocking Lillia's photograph awry as he does so. He then moves to* R *of the table*)

Gino! (*He crosses down* L *of the table*) For God's sake—man—scream and curse, if you can't weep.

(GINO *looks at Philip for the first time since he entered the room*)

Yes, Gino, it's my fault.

(GINO *moves to* R *of Philip. His hand comes foward, hovers over Philip's shoulder like an insect, then descends suddenly, grips Philip's broken arm through the sling and gives it a brutal twist.* PHILIP *cries out in agony and strikes at Gino with all the strength of his free arm. The blow catches Gino off balance. He staggers against the table, knocking over the lamp, which falls to the floor, shatters and goes out. The room is now in darkness, broken by scattered patches of moonlight. From now on, we can distinguish Philip and Gino from one another by their difference in height, but we cannot see their faces; their movements are discernible in a general way, but not in detail*)

(*He gasps with pain*) Damn you! Strike me, if you want—but don't touch my arm.

(GINO *moves towards Philip*)

Gino! Gino! (*He makes a dash above the table towards the arch* C)

SCENE 3   WHERE ANGELS FEAR TO TREAD   53

(GINO, *with the speed and lightness of a cat, moves into the arch* C, *intercepts Philip and again seizes the broken arm.* PHILIP, *with a groan of pain, manages to knock* GINO *down, and he falls back into the loggia.* PHILIP *runs to the couch and lies behind it, down* L. GINO *rises. He has lost Philip momentarily, but he tiptoes through the darkness into the room, pausing occasionally as if to scent his prey, until he is* R *of the couch, then he goes round the couch in a noiseless rush, catching* PHILIP *as he is scrambling to his feet.* GINO *drags Philip* C, *pinions him on his back on the floor and kneels astride him, holding him by the broken arm*)

Christ! (*He gives a thin, wordless scream of suffering that is barely human*)

(GINO *lets go of the broken arm, shifts his position and puts both hands around Philip's throat.* PHILIP'S *sobs begin to grow thick and strangling, as* GINO *tightens his fingers around Philip's windpipe. The last word passes into a sigh, as he loses consciousness.*

CAROLINE *enters up* R *in the loggia, carrying a lighted lantern. She sees the two men and runs into the room*)

CAROLINE. Leave him, Gino. Gino! Leave him! (*She puts the lantern on the table, goes to Gino, stoops over, pulls his hands away from Philip's throat and holds them in her own. In a voice deep with compassion*) Your son is dead, Gino. Your son is dead, you cannot bring him back to life, whatever you do. Get up, get up! (*She pulls Gino to his feet*)

(GINO *does not resist.* CAROLINE *pushes* GINO *into the chair down* R *and holds him down, looking into his eyes as he struggles*)

(*She repeats as though exorcizing him of a devil*) Your son is dead, Gino. What is the good of another death? What is the good of more pain?

(PHILIP *recovers consciousness, opens his eyes and stares dazedly at Gino and Caroline*)

(*She begins to tremble with exhaustion from the struggle but her voice does not falter or lose the note that seems to come from some source greater than herself*) Only one thing matters; you have lost your son. I held him in my arms and closed his eyes. Another death won't bring him back to you.

(GINO *has gradually ceased to struggle against her during the above lines.* PHILIP, *full consciousness restored, moans with pain.* GINO *turns his head and looks at Philip, taking in the writhing body, the face covered with dust and sweat and haggard with suffering.* CAROLINE, *watching closely, sees the dawn of comprehension in* GINO'S *face and knows the crisis is over. She takes her hands from his shoulders, crosses to Philip, kneels above him, lifts the broken arm and puts in on his chest.* PHILIP *moans*)

(*She puts her hands under Philip's shoulders and raises him slightly. To Gino*) Help me to lift him up and lay him on the sofa. Be gentle with him.

(GINO *rises and approaches Philip*)

PHILIP (*in a terrified moan*) Don't let him hurt me.

(GINO *halts and looks questioningly at Caroline*)

CAROLINE. He won't hurt you. All that is over. (*She nods to Gino*) Lift him up—lay him on the sofa.

(GINO *lifts Philip, carries him to the couch and lays him on it.* PHILIP *cries out as Gino puts him down.* GINO *backs away down* L. CAROLINE *rises*)

PHILIP (*with a look of hate at Gino*) Kill him! Kill him for me!

(CAROLINE *moves to Philip, gently wipes his face, then straightens up and looks from Philip to Gino*)

CAROLINE (*to both of them; gravely and sternly*) There is to be no more revenge. This thing stops here.

PHILIP. He is evil!

(PERFETTA *enters down the steps and comes into the room. She carries a small mug of milk*)

PERFETTA. Latte. Latte per il bambino. Latte freschissimo.

CAROLINE (*to Gino*) She does not know, Gino.

PERFETTA (*putting the mug on the table*) Madonna mia—che sucede? (*To Gino. Apologetically*) Sono in ritardo un po', ma . . .

GINO (*interrupting; his voice harsh with pain*) Non importa. Non servira mai piu. (*He recalls Philip's earlier words and repeats them slowly*) "The milk will not be needed now." (*He gives a cry of heartbreak, sinks to his knees and the tears stream down his face*)

(CAROLINE *looks at Perfetta.*

PERFETTA, *not comprehending at all, goes into the loggia, and exits up* R. CAROLINE *crosses to the chair down* R, *sits and holds out her arms to Gino.* GINO *crawls to Caroline, buries his head in her breast and weeps desolately, clinging to her like a child.* CAROLINE *speaks no useless words of consolation. Her arms cradle Gino; her hands stroke him lightly; once she bends down and touches her lips to his forehead. Throughout the scene she has seemed endowed with a strength and majesty that transcend the mortal; and now, she seems more than a woman comforting a man in his grief. Her gestures, the lines of her body, recall the great "pietas", her eyes are those that see the utmost boundaries of sorrow and unimaginable tracts beyond.* PHILIP *watches her from the couch and gradually fear and hate leave his face. He turns his eyes away, and gives a sigh of gratitude.* GINO *has no more tears left, but he remains leaning against Caroline in silence.* CAROLINE *waits a second, then unclasps her arms and touches Gino's cheek*)

CAROLINE. Gino. Gino! The milk will help Philip to recover a little. Take it to him and persuade him to drink it.

(GINO *rises slowly, goes to the table, picks up the mug of milk then turns to look at Caroline.* CAROLINE *nods.* GINO *crosses to Philip. This time,* PHILIP *does not shrink from his touch as* GINO *supports him with one arm as he drinks*)

PHILIP. Thank you.

GINO *sits exhaustedly on the floor by the couch, with his back against it and raises the mug to his lips. He drinks as—*

the LIGHTS *dim to* BLACK-OUT

SCENE 4

SCENE—*The salone of the hotel. Morning, two weeks later.*

When the LIGHTS *come up, it is about eight o'clock. The salone is sunlit.* SIGNORA ALETTI *is behind the desk, making out a bill. She murmurs some of her addition aloud, frowns and strikes out errors.* HARRIET *is seated* L *of the table, which is now against the wall up* C, *writing postcards. She is pale and her bulk seems to have shrunk somewhat, otherwise she looks as she did before her breakdown.*

HARRIET (*looking up*) What is the date?
SIGNORA ALETTI. Scusi?
HARRIET. The day of the month?
SIGNORA ALETTI. Ah—si. La data—it is the twenty-nine Agosto, Miss 'Erriton.
HARRIET. The twenty-ninth? But that's impossible—we arrived here on the twelfth.
SIGNORA ALETTI. Si—si, signorina—but you have stay here more than two weeks.
HARRIET. What? Oh—yes, yes—of course. (*She gathers up her postcards, rises and crosses to the desk*) I—oh . . . (*She frowns, moves to the table, picks up her handbag and returns to the desk*) I would like stamps for these, please. (*She opens her handbag*)
SIGNORA ALETTI (*smiling kindly*) Yes, Miss Herriton. (*She takes a cash-box containing stamps from the shelf under the desk*) How many you wish?
HARRIET. Three. For England. (*Suddenly*) Oh, how silly of me! Never mind.
SIGNORA ALETTI. Scusi?
HARRIET. No stamps. *Niente.* (*She closes her handbag, moves* C *and calls*) Caroline! Caroline!

(SIGNORA ALETTI *shrugs and replaces the box under the desk*)

CAROLINE (*off; upstairs*) Yes, dear—I'm just coming.

(CAROLINE *enters down the stairs and moves to* L *of Harriet.*
SIGNORA ALETTI *exits up* RC)

HARRIET (*holding up the postcards; with an embarrassed little laugh*)

Caroline! Fancy! I wrote three cards to send to Sawston and I've just remembered that we'll get there before they do.

CAROLINE. Why don't you send them, anyway? People always like to get pretty postcards.

HARRIET. It would be foolish to waste the money on stamps. (*With uncharacteristic indecision*) On the other hand, it seems a pity to waste the cards. I found them in my writing-case when I was packing and ... (*She is distracted by a more serious problem that this recalls*) Oh, Caroline! When I came to pack my hot-water bottle, it wasn't there. I searched everywhere but it had simply vanished.

CAROLINE. Didn't you leave it in Paris on your way here?

HARRIET. Of course. (*She sits* R *of the table*) I shouldn't wonder if the *femme de chambre* at that beastly hotel stole it. (*With helpless despair*) Whatever shall I do without it? It's sure to be chilly on the train; they never give one enough blankets.

CAROLINE. I'll try and buy you another, Harriet. I'll go straight to the farmacia and see if they have one in stock.

HARRIET (*with great relief*) Thank you. (*She opens her bag and extracts a coin. Worried*) But you won't have time, will you?

CAROLINE. Plenty. The train doesn't leave for over an hour and my luggage is all packed.

HARRIET. I wish I had finished *my* packing. (*She hands the coin to Caroline*)

CAROLINE. You have finished it, dear. You've only to close your cases.

HARRIET. Oh. But you'll have a look round my room to make sure I've left nothing behind, won't you? I've been shockingly forgetful on this trip.

CAROLINE. Don't worry, Harriet, I will. As soon as I've done your errand. (*She turns to go*)

HARRIET. Errand? What errand?

(PHILIP *enters up* RC *and moves to* R *of Harriet. His arm is in a new sling*)

CAROLINE (*stopping and turning*) I'm going to try and buy you a new hot-water bottle, dear.

HARRIET. Oh, yes, yes—of course. (*She studies one of the postcards*)

(CAROLINE *looks at Philip over Harriet's head*)

(*Suddenly*) How odd! (*She looks up, sees Philip and holds the card out to him*) Look, Philip. Isn't this the same postcard that the Italian sent Irma? Don't you remember—he pretended it came from the baby?

PHILIP (*brusquely*) I remember. (*In a tone of forced, brisk cheerfulness*) All packed, ladies?

HARRIET. I'm not. (*She rises and crosses below Caroline to the stairs*) I'd better go upstairs and finish.

CAROLINE. But, Harriet—you have packed, dear.

(HARRIET *pauses on the stairs and gives a deep, melancholy sigh*)

Scene 4   WHERE ANGELS FEAR TO TREAD

HARRIET. The poor, poor infant. To be taken from us by that tragic accident just when we were all trying so hard to . . . The workings of God are sometimes hard to understand—but we must accept His will—yes, we must accept.

(HARRIET *exits up the stairs.* CAROLINE *sits* L *of the table*)

PHILIP (*to Caroline; with a mixture of revulsion and incredulity*) Is it possible that she really doesn't connect herself with the child's death at all?

CAROLINE. Yes. She began to improve as soon as she ceased to remember her part in what happened. I'm sure once she gets back to Sawston she'll be completely her old self again.

PHILIP. I suppose she will. Nothing—not even this—can change Harriet. But I certainly never dreamed she would get so much better so soon. It's entirely thanks to you.

CAROLINE. I did very little. (*She rises and moves* L)

PHILIP (*collecting his hat from the hooks up* RC) May I come with you to get that hot-water bottle? (*He crosses to* C) Do you realize I've seen almost nothing of you during the last fortnight?

CAROLINE. I would have come to see you oftener at Gino's when he was looking after you, but I didn't like to leave Harriet. Signora Aletti has been wonderfully good about sitting with her, but I do think one of us should always be within call, just in case.

PHILIP. Very well. I take the hint: I'll stay here. (*He moves up* RC *and replaces his hat on the hooks*) In any case, Gino's coming to say good-bye. (*He moves* C)

CAROLINE. Is he? Then you'd better ask Signora Aletti to keep Harriet upstairs while he's here.

PHILIP. Don't worry—I shall. After the way he lied for her at the inquest, the very least I can do is to spare him an encounter with her. Don't be long—he'll want to see you.

(CAROLINE *exits down* L)

(*He crosses to* R, *takes out his wallet, extracts three notes, replaces the wallet in his pocket, then calls*) Signora Aletti! Signora Aletti!

SIGNORA ALETTI (*off*) Un momento, signore. Pronto! Pronto! Mi scusi, signore.

(SIGNORA ALETTI *enters up* R. PHILIP *puts the notes behind his back*)

PHILIP. *Favorisca, signora. E sola, la mia sorella. Vuole* . . .

SIGNORA ALETTI. Ma si, si! Vado e Lei subito. (*She crosses to the stairs, removing her apron and fastening her cuffs*)

PHILIP (*moving* C) *Signora—lei deve fare di tutto de tenerla lei sopra. Il Signor Carella passera qui tra breve e sarebbe molto embarazzante sa la signorina venisse giu.*

SIGNORA ALETTI (*turning to Philip*) Io capisco, signore. Non si preocupi. Io posso distrare Signorina Herriton si Lei ha l'intenzione di venire giu. (*She turns to go upstairs*)

PHILIP. *Lei e stata molto gentile signora con la mia sorella.*

(*The* Signora *makes a deprecating gesture*)

(*He brings the notes from behind his back*) E spero che lei mi permettera di farle un piccolo regalo dalla mia gratitudine.

Signora Aletti (*crossing to* L *of Philip*) No—no—no, signore. Io sono felice di essere stata capace di fare qualche cosa per la sua povera sorella. Per questo—non voglio nulla. (*She gently pushes the notes away, crosses to the stairs and goes up to the second step*)

Philip. Ma non e un pagamento! E solo un segno della mia riconoscenza.

Signora Aletti (*leaning over the banisters*) Caro signore. Mi porti un "English woollie" dell' Inghilterra, quando ritorna a Monteriano.

(Gino *enters down* L)

(*She calls to Gino as she hastens up the stairs*) Buon giorno, Gino.

Gino. Buon giorno, Francesca.

Signora Aletti (*to both*) Arrivederla.

(Signora Aletti *exits up the stairs*)

Gino (*crossing in a melancholy manner to Philip*) Is a lie. (*He removes his hat and shakes hands with Philip*) How can it be a good day when you are leaving?

Philip. I feel just the same, Gino. (*He moves to the chair down* R *and sits*)

Gino (*sitting* R *of the table*) And to think that I could not even pass with you your last evening here. (*He puts his hat on the table*) To think that instead I was forced to pass it in—(*with disgust and contempt*) Poggibonsi.

Philip. How did it go?

Gino (*his melancholy deepening to gloom*) It did not go.

Philip. The lady won't let you off?

Gino. Is her parents. I cannot blame them. It is no concern of theirs that I no longer need a wife.

Philip (*after a pause*) Perhaps it will turn out for the best after all. (*Diffidently*) I hope there will be a child. Soon.

Gino (*brightening slightly*) You will be his godfather?

Philip. I should be honoured.

Gino. If it is a daughter, I will not trouble you. Filippo! If it is a girl perhaps the Signorina Abbott would stand godfather. What do you think?

Philip. I think you'd better write her and ask—if and when the time comes. (*He crosses his legs*)

Gino (*nodding*) I will do so. (*He smiles warmly at Philip and lays a hand on Philip's foot*) But when the time comes she will no longer be Signorina Abbott, no? She will be Signora Philip 'Erriton.

Philip (*rising and crossing to* R *of the stairs*) Don't be a fool.

Gino. I am no fool, I. You are in love with her. It is useless to deny it.

Scene 4 WHERE ANGELS FEAR TO TREAD

PHILIP (*suddenly looking very happy and years younger*) I don't want to deny it.

GINO. Since the night at the teatro it is clear to me. You have not yet asked her to marry you?

PHILIP. I haven't dared even to think that far. (*But hope, remote, dazzling, yet not wholly impossible, lights up his eyes*)

GINO. Well, I advise you to do so, even if she has no money. You are rich, you can afford to overlook the dowry, and this is always pleasing to a woman.

PHILIP (*moving to* L *of the table; with a boyishness totally unlike him*) Do you think she has guessed—what you have guessed?

(GINO *considers then shakes his head doubtfully*)

GINO. With the Signorina Abbott it is difficult to tell. She is not as other women—she is without vanity. A saint. But also very beautiful. (*He rises and moves to* R *of Philip*) I would like to say good-bye to her. Ask her, please, if she will be so kind as to descend.

PHILIP. I'm sorry, Gino, but she's gone out to do an errand for my sister.

(GINO *stiffens very slightly at* "*my sister*")

GINO (*a little formally*) The Signorina Herriton finds herself better now?

PHILIP. Much better, thank you. Almost recovered, in fact.

GINO (*with an uneasy glance towards the staircase; sincerely*) That is good. I hope very soon she is all well.

PHILIP (*with quiet gratitude*) That's very kind of you, Gino.

GINO (*after a pause*) Filippo, you will understand, will you not, why I do not wait and accompany you to the stazione? Much as I would like to, but . . .

PHILIP. My dear fellow, of course I understand.

GINO. Give to Signorina Abbott my most warm wishes. And bring her back with you when you return in the spring.

PHILIP. I—I'll do my utmost.

GINO. You will not fail to return? I will meet you in Siena and we will stay there two—three days at the best hotel. (*In explanation*) I can afford it by then. My new wife bring a little money with her. (*His spirits rising*) But we will not take the ladies for those three days. It will be gayer—just you and I.

PHILIP. Fine! We'll paint the town red.

GINO. Si, si. But at my expense. It is understood that you pay for nothing.

PHILIP (*gravely*) It is understood. *Tante grazie.*

GINO (*embracing Philip on both cheeks*) Arrividerci, fra Filippo.

PHILIP. *Arrividerci*, Gino. I shall miss you.

GINO (*picking up his hat*) Write to me. Siena—don't forget.

(GINO *gently touches Philip's broken arm, then crosses and exits down* L,

E

with a gay wave of his hat. PHILIP *smiles affectionately, looks up at the clock, takes his watch from his pocket and looks at it, then replaces it and turns down* L.

CAROLINE *enters down* L., *carrying a stone hot-water bottle.* PHILIP'S *conversation with Gino has made him shy and he greets Caroline with almost a schoolboy awkwardness*)

PHILIP. Hello. Did you run into Gino? He was just here.
CAROLINE. I saw him but he didn't see me.
PHILIP. Oh! Why didn't you stop him? He particularly wanted to say good-bye to you—he was distressed to miss you.
CAROLINE. He looked in very high spirits.
PHILIP. Yes. He's made me promise to come back to visit him in the spring.
CAROLINE. Has he? He has already ceased to mind about the child.
PHILIP. Oh, no, you're wrong. He minds. Far more than you or I do. But he's honest. He knows that the things that made him happy once will probably make him happy again, and he isn't ashamed to admit it.

(CAROLINE *crosses to the foot of the stairs*)

Don't go yet. (*He moves to* R *of Caroline*) There's something I must tell you. I'm not going back to Sawston or to my mother.
CAROLINE. What are you going to do?
PHILIP. Move to London and try to get a job, a real job with a firm of architects.
CAROLINE. Have you told Mrs Herriton yet?
PHILIP. I wrote her a few days ago. She'll make a fuss, but it can't be helped. So those are my plans, London and work—what are yours?
CAROLINE. Sawston and work.
PHILIP. You can't.
CAROLINE. Of course I can. There's my father, don't forget, and I have a hundred other ties; my district work, my evening classes . . .
PHILIP (*moving* C) But this is nonsense. You must live among people who will appreciate you for what you really are. You can't go back to that hole. I mind for myself as well as for you—I want to see you often.
CAROLINE (*moving to* L *of Philip*) We'll meet whenever you come down from London.
PHILIP. Each with half a dozen stuffy relatives around us. No, thank you. Anyway, even if you wanted to go back to the old death-in-life, and I can't believe you do, it's not possible now. So much has happened.
CAROLINE. I know.
PHILIP. Not only pain and sorrow, but wonderful things.
CAROLINE. All the wonderful things are over.

Scene 4   WHERE ANGELS FEAR TO TREAD   61

PHILIP. I don't believe it. The most wonderful things may be to come.
CAROLINE. All the wonderful things are over. We are just where we were.
PHILIP. Miss Abbott, what's the matter with you? I thought I understood you and I don't. Those first few days here I saw why you had come and why you changed sides. The night you saved Gino and me was a turning-point in my life. I saw your miraculous courage and pity—I've felt differently and have wanted to live differently ever since. And now you tell me that nothing's changed or can change.
CAROLINE. I was talking of myself. I am glad you are going to break away from Sawston. I am sure your new life will be happier than the old one.
PHILIP. Not when I think of you still buried there. You're being evasive with me. You've given me no reason, no real reason why you're going back to all the things you despise. Mediocrity, spitefulness, insensibility. I'm quoting your own words.
CAROLINE (*turning away* L) I must go up to Harriet.
PHILIP (*crossing below Caroline to* L *of her*) I won't let you shut me up. (*He takes the hot-water bottle from her*) You've been frank with me too long to turn aloof and secretive now.
CAROLINE (*crossing to* R) It's a temptation not to be secretive.

(PHILIP *puts the hot-water bottle on the table and moves* RC)

I've wanted to tell you—there is nobody else I can tell, certainly. It would be a relief even though you were embarrassed and perhaps disgusted.
PHILIP. Are you lonely? Is that what it is?
CAROLINE. Yes. So lonely because I can't have what I want that it doesn't matter where I live or what I do. I think you know already.
PHILIP. Perhaps I do. (*He crosses slowly to* L *of her*) But until you say the words I can't believe it.
CAROLINE. It's true—I love him. I love Gino and I'm going to Sawston and if I mayn't talk to you sometimes about him I shall die.
PHILIP. Of course you may. I love him, too.
CAROLINE. You are misunderstanding. I'm in love with him. Crudely. Get over supposing I'm refined. That's what confuses you. Get over it. (*She pauses*) Why don't you say something? Why don't you laugh at me?
PHILIP. Laugh?
CAROLINE. Yes, tell me I'm a fool or worse. Say all you said to Lillia—that he's vulgar and mercenary, ruthless with women, the son of an Italian dentist with a handsome face. That's the sort of help I want. You don't enter life, you look on it as a spectacle. You told me so yourself.
PHILIP. That was before.
CAROLINE. A spectacle that's either beautiful or funny. And

this is funny, isn't it? Isn't it really funny? (*She sits in the chair down* R, *facing front*) Help me. I love Gino and I'm not ashamed of it. I'll never see him again and there's nothing I ever want to see again except his face.

PHILIP. Well, as you say, it's a very handsome face. But *loin des yeux*, you know. This may be what the books call a passing fancy.

CAROLINE. No, because I daren't risk seeing him. If I did, if I saw him often I might be cured. The things I dislike about him might come to matter.

PHILIP. Or he might get fat.

CAROLINE. You are treating it just as I hoped. Go on.

PHILIP. There's the obvious fact that you and he have nothing whatsoever in common.

CAROLINE. Nothing except the times we've had together. I suppose it all began that very first morning when I went to his house. I didn't realize it then—but when I did I prayed that we should all remain just as we were: Gino with the child he loved, and you and I and Harriet gone away, so that I should never have to see him or speak to him again. But we stayed.

PHILIP. Yes—we stayed.

CAROLINE. Stop blaming yourself. From the very first morning I longed for him. But all through he looked on me as a sort of goddess. I who would have given myself to him at any time.

(SIGNORA ALETTI *enters at the top of the stairs. She sees Caroline and registers relief*)

SIGNORA ALETTI (*coming down the stairs*) Ah, Signorina Abbott. L'altra Signorina desidera che Lei venga sopra . . .

CAROLINE (*interrupting*) Vado a lei, signora. (*She rises*)

SIGNORA ALETTI (*crossing and going behind the desk*) Bene. Grazie, signorina.

CAROLINE (*to Philip*) I must go now and help Harriet fasten her cases. (*She crosses to the stairs*)

PHILIP (*picking up the hot-water bottle*) You're forgetting this. (*He moves to Caroline*)

CAROLINE (*pausing and turning*) Oh, yes. The hot-water bottle.

(PHILIP *hands the hot-water bottle to Caroline*)

PHILIP. You are right—the wonderful things are over. But they may save us, yet. They've left behind something indestructible—something that once given can never be taken away.

(CAROLINE *looks at Philip as though considering what he has said and permitting him to develop it*)

(*He cannot trust himself to continue*) Thank you. Thank you for everything.

(CAROLINE *exits up the stairs*)

(*He watches Caroline out of sight, then crosses to the desk and pulls his wallet from his pocket*) Signora—il mio conto per favore.

Signora Aletti. Si, signore, e pronto. Ho fatto tutto in sieme, per Lei e per la sua sorella. Grazie tante!

Curtain

FURNITURE AND PROPERTY LIST

(The Ground Plans have been adapted from the original Sets which were designed for use with a revolving stage)

ACT I

Scene 1

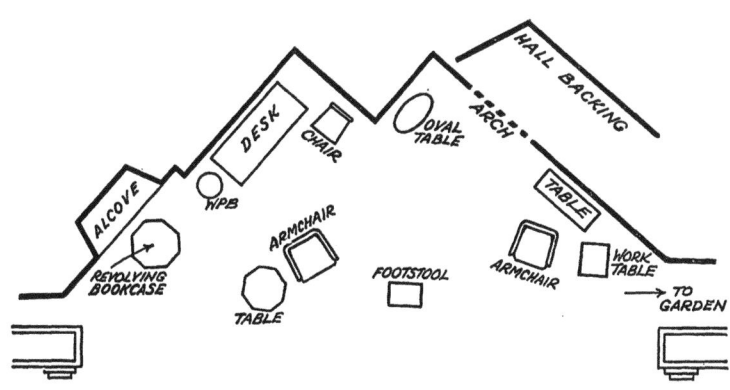

On stage: Revolving bookcase (R)
  On it: silver ashtray and match-stand, 2 silver-framed pictures
  In it: 1906 period *Bradshaw*, books, music books, period *Punch* magazines, newspapers
  In alcove R: blue china bowl and palm
  Moorish table (RC) *On it:* silver-framed photograph, silver sweet dish, silver smelling-salts bottle
  Mahogany Victorian armchair (RC)
  Desk. *On it:* writing-paper, silver inkstand and pens, 2 library books, silver-framed photograph, silver vase with sweet peas, carriage clock, small framed photograph, oil lamp (*not practical*), double silver-framed photograph, silver blotter
  Waste-paper basket (R of desk)
  Small oval table (up LC) *On it:* oval silver-framed photograph. silver vase with flowers
  Wooden armchair with brocaded seat (up C)
  Green-covered footstool (down C)
  Mahogany Victorian armchair (L)
  Mahogany Victorian work-table (down L) *In it:* sewing for Mrs Herriton, threaded needle and cotton, reels of cotton, rolls of coloured tape

WHERE ANGELS FEAR TO TREAD 65

Table (L) *On it:* palm in pot
On walls: gold-framed pictures
Carpet and rugs on floor
In arch: blue velvet curtains

Off stage (down L): Trug basket. *In it:* cut flowers (MRS HERRITON)
Cutters (MRS HERRITON)
Down stage (*up* R): Coloured postcard (IRMA)
2 library books (HARRIET)

Personal: MRS HERRITON: gardening gloves, hat, handkerchief, gold-rimmed spectacles in hanging belt case
PHILIP: cigarettes in case, cigarette holder, matches, gold pocket watch
HARRIET: handbag

SCENE 2

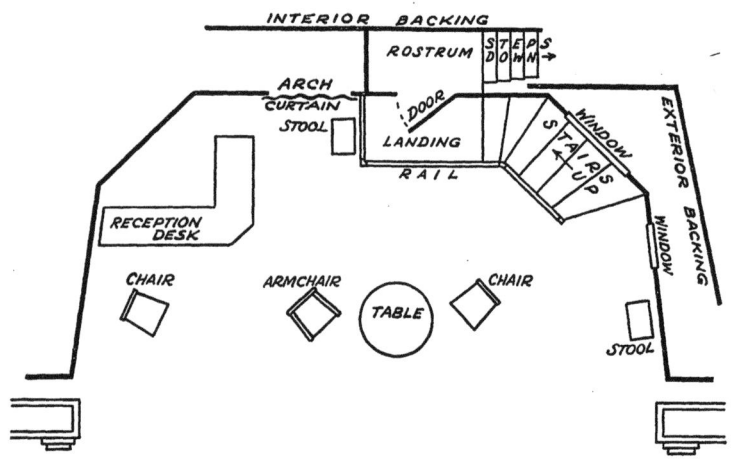

On stage: Upright chair with rush seat (down R)
Reception desk. *On it:* gramophone with horn speaker, 2 Italian magazines, pen, inkstand, brass ashtray, account ledger, pencil, hotel stationery, begonia plant in china pot, china jug with water, hand press bell (*not working*), pile of gramophone records
Under it: waste-paper basket
On wall behind desk: key-rack with keys, single gas bracket, clock, letter-rack with letters, calendar, coloured picture of Victor Emmanuel in red velvet frame
Red curtain and brass rod for doorway up RC

Small stool-table (up RC)
On wall over stool: rack of coat-hooks
On wall up C: double gas bracket with chains, picture of Santa Deodata in gold frame
Marble-topped table (C)
Rush-seated armchair (R of table) *On it:* fan
Rush-seated upright chair (L of table)
On staircase bracket: oil lamp
On staircase wall: gold-framed picture of towers and hills as postcard in Scene 1
Shutters for windows
Stool (L)
On wall L: brass wall-vase with dried flowers
Window shutters closed
Light fittings on

Off stage (down L): 2 suitcases, 1 with lady's umbrella strapped to it (CAB DRIVER)
Lady's red dressing-case (CAB DRIVER)
Off stage (up R): Tray. *On it:* carafe of white wine, glass (SIGNORA ALETTI)

Personal: PHILIP: hat, handkerchief, sling, splints and bandage, coins
HARRIET: handkerchief, handbag, gloves

SCENE 3

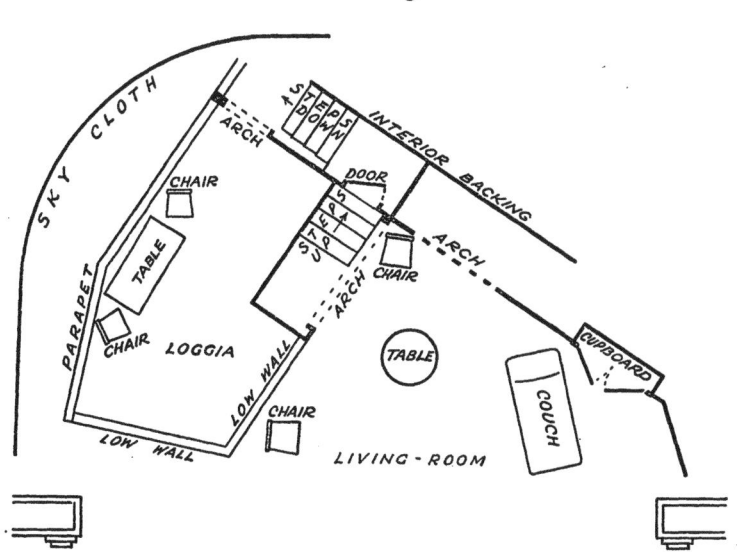

On stage: In loggia: wooden table. *On it:* wooden ashtray full of cigar ends, cup and saucer, plate, china dish, china mug, painted tin coffee-pot
2 wooden chairs (dusty)

In room: Wheel-back wooden chair (down R) *On it:* pair of dark trousers with braces
Table (C) *On it:* metal ashtray full of cigar ends, tin plate
Ladder-back chair (up C) *On it:* pile of Italian newspapers, piece of yellow striped material
In arch: red curtain
Behind arch: hip-bath, sponge in bath
Horsehair couch.
  On it: roll pillow, red wool scarf
  Under it: pair of old boots, pair of grey socks
  Beside it: guitar
  L *of couch:* large basket with pillow, blanket, baby doll wrapped in white woollen shawl
Shelf over archway: On it: hanging jug, metal meat cover, brass jug, china tobacco jar, small haversack, long-haired brush end
On back wall: picture of Lillia in black frame, draped with black crêpe, test tube of dried flowers
Small rug (under table C)
Built-in cupboard and shelves
  On top shelf: Italian newspapers, red jug
  On second shelf: newspapers, rags, glass vase, 2 small flower-pots, empty clear long-necked wine bottle
  On third shelf: 2 candles, large flower-pot, 4 wax spills
  On bottom shelf: tin, razor, shaving soap and brush, china candlestick, glass bowl with scissors and hair clippers, painted china jug
  On protruding part of cupboard: night light, candle, wooden box with newspapers, green china flower-pot, long-necked brown wine bottle
  Inside cupboard doors: old postcards pinned on, torn picture of Victor Emmanuel
  In cupboard top shelf: straw hat, black and gold square, cream lace shawl, man's light checked trousers, 2 woollen tartan squares, pair long fawn stockings, fawn waistcoat
  On second shelf: yellow shirt, green shirt, while silk shirt, blue twill jacket, piece of white linen, piece of yellow striped material
  On bottom shelf: old fawn raincoat

68 WHERE ANGELS FEAR TO TREAD

Off stage: Copper can with water (GINO)
  Tray. *On it:* 3 glasses, plate of cakes, tin with 2 cigars, loose matches (PERFETTA)
  Glass decanter of white wine (GINO)

Personal: GINO: lit cigar, hat, packet of soap (in jacket pocket)
  CAROLINE: hat, handbag, gloves
  PHILIP: hat, bandage, splints, sling

ACT II

SCENE 1

Setting as Act I, Scene 2

Strike: Record from gramophone

Set: Time-table on shelf under desk
  Red swag round picture of Santa Deodata
  Small vase of flowers under picture
  Armchair in place R of table C
  Fan on stool L
  Magazines on desk
  Caroline's key on key-board
Window shutters open
Light fittings off

Personal: CAROLINE: key, hat, handbag, gloves, parasol
  PHILIP: bandage, splints, sling, hat, cigarettes in case, cigarette holder, matches
  HARRIET: hat, handbag, gloves
  GINO: hat, lit cigar, matches

SCENE 2

Setting as previous Scene
Shutters open
Light fittings on

Off stage: Whip (CAB DRIVER)

Personal: HARRIET: note in envelope
  SIGNORA ALETTI: programme, fan, evening bag
  CAROLINE: programme, stole, evening bag
  PHILIP: programme, bandage, splints, sling

Scene 3

Setting as Act I, Scene 3

Strike: Baby and shawl from basket
Bath
China from loggia table
Trousers from chair in room L

Set: *On table* C: oil lamp (dim)

Off stage: Lighted lantern (CAROLINE)
Mug of milk (PERFETTA)

Personal: GINO: cane, hat, gloves
CAROLINE: stole
PHILIP: bandage, splints, sling

Scene 4

Setting as Act II, Scene 2

Strike: Swag and flowers from picture
Begonia from desk
Move table C back to wall up C

Set: *On table up* C: inkwell, pen, 3 postcards, Harriet's handbag. *In it:* coins
On desk: pot of geraniums, bill forms
Under desk: cash-box with block of Italian stamps
On hooks up R: Philip's hat

Off stage: Stone hot-water bottle (CAROLINE)

Personal: SIGNORA ALETTI: tea-towel as apron
GINO: hat
CAROLINE: handkerchief
PHILIP: watch, new sling, wallet with paper money

LIGHTING PLOT

Property fittings required: double gas bracket, single gas bracket, 2 oil lamps, 1 lantern

ACT I, SCENE 1

    Interior. A small room

    THE APPARENT SOURCE OF LIGHT is daylight

    THE MAIN ACTING AREAS cover the whole setting

To open: Effect of bright sunshine

Cue 1	MRS HERRITON exits at end of Scene *Dim* LIGHTS *to* BLACK-OUT	(Page 16)

ACT I, SCENE 2. Evening

    Interior. An hotel salone

    THE APPARENT SOURCES OF LIGHT are, in daytime, two windows L, and at night, a double gas bracket C, a single gas bracket R and an oil lamp up L

    THE MAIN ACTING AREAS are R, C, and L

Cue 2	When Scene set *Bring up* LIGHTS *for evening effect* *Bring in all fittings* *Blue outside windows and off down* L	(Page 16)
Cue 3	SIGNORA ALETTI turns down gas bracket C *Dim out gas bracket up* C *Dim out covering lights*	(Page 17)
Cue 4	CAB DRIVER turns up gas bracket C *Bring up gas bracket up* C *Bring up covering lights*	(Page 17)
Cue 5	PHILIP turns out gas bracket up R *Dim out gas bracket up* R *Dim out covering lights*	(Page 26)
Cue 6	PHILIP turns out gas bracket C *Dim out gas bracket up* C *Dim out covering lights*	(Page 26)
Cue 7	PHILIP exits up the stairs *Dim* LIGHTS *to* BLACK-OUT	(Page 26)

ACT I, SCENE 3. Morning

    Interior/Exterior. A loggia R and a living-room L

    THE APPARENT SOURCES OF LIGHT are, in daytime, natural light; and at night, moonlight R and an oil lamp on the table C of the living-room L

    THE MAIN ACTING AREAS are R, RC, LC, and L

Cue 8   When Scene set   (Page 27)
       Bing up LIGHTS *for effect of bright sunshine*

ACT II, SCENE 1. Noon

The hotel salone

To open: Effect of bright sunshine

Cue 9   PHILIP exits up RC   (Page 47)
       Dim LIGHTS *to* BLACK-OUT

ACT II, SCENE 2. Night

The hotel salone

Cue 10   SIGNORA ALETTI sings off L   (Page 47)
       Bring in evening lighting
       Gas bracket up C, *dim*
       Oil lamp on stairs, on
       Gas bracket up R, *on*
       Moonlight through windows

Cue 11   SIGNORA ALETTI turns up gas bracket C   (Page 48)
       Bring up gas bracket up C *to full*
       Bring up covering lights

Cue 12   HARRIET: "... her and stole ..."   (Page 51)
       Dim LIGHTS *to* BLACK-OUT

ACT II, SCENE 3. Night

Gino's house

Cue 13   When Scene set   (Page 51)
       Bring up LIGHTS *for exterior moonlight and shadow effect, and dim lamplight in room* L

Cue 14   GINO turns up lamp in room L   (Page 52)
       Bring up lamp in room L
       Bring up covering lights

Cue 15   GINO knocks lamp over   (Page 52)
       Snap out lamp
       Snap out covering lights

Cue 16	CAROLINE enters with lantern *Bring up lights in room* L	(Page 53)
Cue 17	GINO drinks *Dim* LIGHTS *to* BLACK-OUT	(Page 55)

ACT II, SCENE 4. Morning

The hotel salone

Cue 18	When Scene set *Bring up* LIGHTS *for effect of bright sunshine*	(Page 55)

EFFECTS PLOT

ACT I

Scene 1

Cue 1	Mrs Herriton: ". . . the time being." *Piano scales*	(Page 13)
Cue 2	Mrs Herriton: ". . . her of him." *Piano ceases*	(Page 14)
Cue 3	Mrs Herriton: ". . . him up immoral." *Czerny piano exercises*	(Page 14)
Cue 4	Mrs Herriton: ". . . get it for me." *Piano ceases*	(Page 14)
Cue 5	Mrs Herriton: ". . . very tactful handling." *Schumann's "Merry Peasant" on piano*	(Page 15)
Cue 6	Mrs Herriton: "Miss Maynard!" *Piano ceases*	(Page 15)
Cue 7	Mrs Herriton puts *Bradshaw* in bookcase *Czerny piano exercises*	(Page 15)
Cue 8	During Scene change *Cross fade Czerny exercises to recording of Caruso singing "O Paradiso" from "L'Africaine" by Meyerbeer. This continues when Scene 2 commences*	(Page 16)

Scene 2

Cue 9	Signora Aletti stops gramophone *Stop music*	(Page 17)
Cue 10	Philip exits up the stairs *Church bell strikes ten*	(Page 26)

Scene 3

Cue 11*	Gino: "Un momento." *Baby squeals angrily*	(Page 32)
Cue 12*	Gino: ". . . Signorina Inglese?" *Baby squeals*	(Page 33)

* These can be done by the actress playing Caroline.

ACT II

Scene 1

No cues

Scene 2

Cue 13 At end of Scene (Page 51)
         Church bell strikes 12

Scene 3

No cues

Scene 4

No cues